Tell You What

Tell You What
Great New Zealand Nonfiction 2016

Edited by Susanna Andrew
& Jolisa Gracewood

AUCKLAND
UNIVERSITY
PRESS

First published 2015

Auckland University Press
University of Auckland
Private Bag 92019
Auckland 1142
New Zealand
www.press.auckland.ac.nz

ISBN 978 1 86940 844 2

Publication is assisted by
ARTS COUNCIL OF NEW ZEALAND TOI AOTEAROA

A catalogue record for this book is available from the National Library
of New Zealand

Cover design: Philip Kelly Studio

Printed by Printlink Ltd, Wellington

Contents

Foreword:
John Campbell

When I was a student in English at Victoria University, we were asked, during a tutorial in one of those anaesthetisingly bland rooms in the von Zedlitz Building, what New Zealand culture consisted of.

An absence, it seemed.

I'm ashamed to say our answers were miserable. And wrong. In the years since, I've returned often (in my head, and on paper) to that room, and to our flaccid and ignorant sense that life was elsewhere. And when I try to understand my naivety, my cultural cringe, my pettiness, I put it down, in part, to received wisdom.

In a way, we'd appropriated Allen Curnow's famous couplet (so memorable, and so good) into a kind of tea-towel homily of national identity: 'Not I, some child, born in a marvellous year, / Will learn the trick of standing upright here.'

But Curnow had written that in 1943. And four decades later, by the time our tutorial fecklessly reheated it, as robotically as times-table rote, people had stood upright in the middle of the field at Rugby Park, Hamilton, or marched upright against the Springbok Tour on Molesworth Street, or on winter motorways, or directly into the batons of the Red Squad. And Norman Kirk had sent frigates to Mururoa. And Marilyn Waring was about to stand upright to cross the floor of Parliament. And Whina Cooper's hīkoi had reached Parliament, 1000 kilometres of upright in their wake. And Bill

Manhire's sixth poetry collection was being published, words upright in new ways. And Janet Frame was miraculously upright. And Flying Nun was up and upright in op-shop pants. And people had been dragged from Bastion Point, flat upright. And our dissent was palpable. And our anger was palpable. And our bullies were vicious and larger than life. And people were upright, everywhere.

Perhaps what we didn't have yet were enough writers to decipher that. To explain it. To take the failing narrative of our uncertain infancy, our shallow-rooted identity, and assert the roots that dissent was planting. To observe that we had learned Curnow's trick. That anger, and a belief in the urgent need for something better, had made us stand.

I received this book as a manuscript. A4, which is never as good as a real book, evoking, as it does, bank statements, electricity bills, and those group letters from a distant relative whose children are all so spit-combed and exceptional that the annual Christmas missive provokes a terrible desire to climb into the oven beside the turkey.

But even in A4, it was fantastic in its stridency, its 'oi' confidence, its talent, and its pluralism. 'Hey Curnow! Hey, John Campbell and your shit-lazy Vic Uni Class! Tell You What!'

So, what?

That's the thing, of course, there isn't one single, defining 'what'. There is no prescribed us-ness. No tutorial delineation of a defining national voice. There are, instead, multitudinous voices. Defying prescription and formula. A true self-confidence, beyond hopefulness and latency, now deep in the bones. There is also something of Walt Whitman here: 'I celebrate myself, and sing myself', and the wonderful lines that come later in that great poem: 'Behold, I do not give lectures or a little charity, / When I give I give myself.'

It's unfair to single only some people out. But the poets Ashleigh Young and Kate Camp bring a dancing love of words to their nonfiction, while Kirsten McDougall turns the 'non' rather wonderfully on its head:

> It is hard to bring the real self into view – we turn to metaphor, to fiction for such tasks – we are forced to use artifice and craft. How contradictory we are!

Yes.

And Elizabeth Knox, who I admire for the rich vastness of her prose, for how her writer's brain tentacles into everywhere, sends a two-page telegram that is so supremely good and timely that every time I re-read it, it astounds and delights me afresh.

Nicky Hager writes 'I love the work of investigative journalism' and then reminds us of its vital importance, its obstacles and its costs. Both local and international in its view, and singularly (and sadly) nonfiction, Hager's truth evokes C. K. Stead's fictional sense, in *Smith's Dream*, of what a bully the state can be.

Giovanni Tiso reveals a rigorous tenderness. Tina Makereti glides with us, as if writing was effortless for her (which suggests a great deal of effort). Steve Braunias is as evocative as ever, and compelling, as he so often is. Ali Ikram contributes a wise and winking story that I am pleased to hear again. Vicki Anderson writes vividly from Christchurch, in parts as unflinching as a fluorescent light, but never heartlessly. She is very good indeed. I want to read more by her. And by Kristen Ng.

But then, there are no weak links here. Everything stands in this 'marvellous year'. A diaspora of words, in a fine, New Zealand collection. Take it and read, as, one by one, each writer tells us their what. And our what. And what.

Kirsten McDougall
A Small Candle, An Elk

. . . how can man 'know himself'? He is a thing obscure and veiled: if the hare have seven skins, man can cast from him seventy times seven, and yet will not be able to say 'Here art thou in very truth; this is outer shell no more.' Also this digging into one's self, this straight, violent descent into the pit of one's being, is a troublesome and dangerous business to start. A man may easily take such hurt, that no physician can heal him. – Friedrich Nietzsche, from *Schopenhauer as Educator*

One morning as I was trying desperately to leave the house for work, shouting at the kids to get their jackets bags shoes on, I ran back to the bedroom to grab my watch and was brought to a halt by a sharp stench. I smelt shit. Cat shit.

This was not the first time our elderly blind cat had toileted under the bed so I immediately knew what the foul smell was. She did it one Saturday a few weeks ago when David and I were sitting in bed, drinking tea and reading. She walked into the bedroom, gave a doleful moan of a meow to announce herself, crawled under the bed and squatted. I couldn't hear the piss hitting my yoga mat, stored under the bed, but as soon as I could smell the pungent ammonia which seemed to be rising in waves, like heat rises off the road in summer,

First published on 10 July 2014 on Kirsten's blog The Invisible Writer: invisiblerider.wordpress.com my mind's eye could also see how the piss pooled and ran along the folds of the mat to spill on to the wooden boards beneath. I leapt out of bed to stop her, to stop the piss from running everywhere. My lie-in was ruined. My mood, instantly vile.

Since that morning we'd tried to get into the habit of closing the bedroom door. Keep the cat out. If it looked like she was in an urgent way, sniffing here and there around the bathroom door and around our bedroom door, I put her outside. I couldn't handle the thought of a kitty litter tray inside. It's only a few years since we'd gotten away from children in nappies, surely the cat could look after her own needs? But no, the cat could not. And now I'd forgotten to shut the door and she had done five stinky logs and pissed on one of the overnight bags we also kept under the bed.

I ran down the hall, the bag dripping piss on the wooden boards as I went, opened the back door and threw the bag outside. Then I grabbed the cat who was sitting in the morning sun contentedly cleaning her paws. I picked her up and put her blind elderly cat nose right up to her shit, which had rolled off the bag when I'd thrown it and lay on the concrete path just outside our door. The children watched with interest.

'What's that?' the smallest said, pointing at the shit.

'Cat shit,' I said.

'Don't say shit, Mummy,' said the eldest. The youngest tittered.

'Sorry. It's poo, it's cat poo,' I said.

'Why is it on my bag?' said the youngest.

'It's my bag too,' said the eldest.

'Stormy did it there,' I said. 'She . . .' I wanted to explain why she did it on their overnight bag, but I couldn't because I didn't know why.

'Ewww,' said the youngest, and started to do some fake crying.

'Please don't make that noise,' I said. I was, by this time, quite frustrated and couldn't handle the fake-crying child. 'I'm going to clean it up.'

The cat was outside now and I shut the door on her and locked her cat door so she couldn't get back in. I cleaned up the mess, and wrote a note to David telling him not, under any circumstance, to let the cat in. Then we left for the day, the kids and me. The cat was locked outside.

When I got home the cat was once again inside. David said it was too cold for her to be outside all day, she didn't know what she was doing, she was an elderly cat, couldn't we just take more care and shut the bedroom door? I looked for the rage I'd felt in the morning, found the residue and put the cat outside again. I could close the bedroom door, but the cat must pay.

Half an hour later, my pity for the old cat, and a slow growing shame at what I'd done crawled in and replaced my rage. I opened the door for her. She sat at the top of the hall facing down towards the bedroom. I made a noise deep in my throat and growled at her. She turned and walked away from me.

Part of my 'punishment' to the cat was to shame her – to put her face close up to her own shit, and to growl at her, and to make her sit outside the family home. I don't know whether the cat was actually ashamed. In a way, her reaction is unimportant. What mattered, in the heat of the moment, was that my anger at her adding to my jobs to do before I left the house, my disgust at the shit and smell in my bedroom, and my dismay that she be doing this to us (yes to us, not to herself) after thirteen years of care – all this needed to be answered.

I wanted to shame the cat, but the consequence of my reaction meant I was feeling ashamed of myself.

The rational part of me knows that what I did to her, to punish her, is wrongheaded, with an edge of cruelty, and will not change her behaviour. She is an old cat, she is blind, the outdoors probably frightens her – it's cold and she can only feel her way around our garden. She knows our garden because she's lived there most of her sighted life, but still. What I did to her I did because I was angry and wanted to take my anger out on her, to offload it, and my immediate reaction (aside from physical torment or torture, which even I won't do) was to shame her.

My reaction was thoughtless – indeed, reactionary. I was acting out a learnt behaviour, one that goes all the way back to my own childhood, to the ways in which I was punished for my own 'naughty behaviour'. When I was small I was hit for 'being naughty'; this was how children were punished back then. Punishment was physical and often involved the wooden spoon. The wooden spoon was broken against my tender backside a few times. There was something subversively wonderful if my butt managed to break the wooden handle. It hurt, but it was almost worth it to ruin the implement that hurt me so. I would then be 'told off' and asked to think about my actions. Did the person doing the hitting, my mother, feel ashamed as I did after the cat shit incident; as I do after yelling with anger at my own children for things they do that displease me?

After being hit, I would be embarrassed, sometimes I would feel guilt for having done what I'd done; I would be ashamed. Clinical psychologist Gershen Kaufman wrote a book I'm reading in an attempt to understand what I'm doing, why it is I'm writing this down. Kaufman's book is called *The*

Psychology of Shame. He believes that feelings such as guilt and embarrassment arise out of shame. Kaufman argues that shame is the home base of many negative 'affects' such as guilt, self-consciousness, embarrassment, shyness, discouragement, a sense of failure and of inferiority. These are feelings in themselves, but they all arise out of and can be traced back to the base affect of shame. When I was hit with the wooden spoon the intention was perhaps to shame me, to make me feel that I would not repeat the 'naughty behaviour'.

I disagree with physical punishment. I think that hitting children shows a lack of control, it does nothing to help the child understand why what they've done is wrong and why they shouldn't do it and it makes a child fear the adult who is supposed to protect and love them. But shame is important in development. It is part of how we learn to control our behaviour. Kaufman writes that 'Shame plays a vital role in the development of conscience. By alerting us to misconduct or wrongdoing – to transgression in whatever form – shame motivates necessary self-correcting.'

Self-correction; isn't that what we want our children to learn? And our cats? But there's a point at which shame overwhelms the self, and becomes problematic.

I lied. I wrote that I discovered the cat shit after I went back into the bedroom to get my watch. This is a detail about which only David would know the truth, and even then, he probably wouldn't notice. My watch will always be found on the shelf above the kitchen sink, where I place it carefully after I take it off to wash the dishes. Most nights I do the dishes because David does most of the cooking. If you cook you don't have to wash up, that's our rule.

My watch was my grandfather's. My father gave it to me. It's a 'gold' watch, a Certina automatic Club 2000, inscribed on the back: 'Presented to H.E. McDougall 30 Yrs Service Caltex Oil (NZ) Limited.' (Why was it necessary for them to inscribe 'Limited'? What kind of pedant inscribed that on this watch?) I know exactly where I put the watch. I'm careful with it.

The real reason I went back to the bedroom, whereupon I discovered the cat shit, was to spray some more hairspray in my hair. It was flat and greasy, and I hadn't bothered to wash it and I was hopeful that some hairspray might mask the way it looked. I'd already sprayed it, but I wanted to spray it some more. There was no point to the hairspray as I was about to put on my bike helmet and ride for thirty sweaty minutes to work. But I did it anyway.

So why did I lie and say that I went back to the bedroom to get my watch?

Vanity. My own shame about vanity. Shame about the greasiness of my hair, as if the production of sebum in my scalp, the way it darkened the strands and made them lie flat against my head, said something of my own human weakness. A line in a Geoff Cochrane poem got seared into my brain when I first read it: 'Odours of sebum and dust. The couch's fabric had a bummy, sebaceous smell.' My hair is oily, unwashed, bummy. By not washing it I show my own decay, I reveal my own base animal smell. I see my unwashed hair as ugly hair. God forbid I be seen as ugly. Ugly people with greasy hair should cover their heads and hide their faces – no one wants to see them.

This is why I lied about the watch and the hairspray. There is a façade I must keep up; a well-groomed elegance, an ironed shirt, clean hair, rimmed eyes, a hint of blush on the cheek, of red in the lip. I craft myself, as much as – no, more – than I attempt to craft my writing. Strangely, I would let writing slip before I'd ever let my appearance 'go'. I can almost hear the woman who says, in a voice that sounds just like my mother, a hand held to the mouth, the tone lowered, 'She's really let herself go.' Where? I want to ask. To where did she let her self go?

How vain I am. How deep my shame lives within me. How, despite my demands for honesty, my contempt of fakery in other people and in things, my reading and learning, my almost forty years of living, I am wedded to artifice – to creating a wall to hide my shame behind. I am a cut and pasted work of fiction.

I should like to imagine that the candlelight of my real self is flickering in an underground cave, but this would be to suppose the self as an unchanging thing, a lump of wax slowly melting, a wick long enough to last a lifetime – but easy enough to snuff out given a stray air current, pinched fingers, a breath. While it burns it lights up the marks on the wall of the cave, made by the hands of early humans 27,000 years ago. Those spirit animals move and change in the flickering light – bison charge, elk leap on the walls.

It is hard to bring the real self into view – we turn to metaphor, to fiction, for such tasks – we are forced to use artifice and craft. How contradictory we are! Art to expose our fictive selves, metaphor to dig beyond that self in our attempts to find what is real.

If the core of the self is a small candle, to bring this out of the cave would be to diminish its light under the sun's brilliant rays. It would be dangerous. It is best it stays out of the wind and rain, in the sheltered climate of the cave, no human breath to atrophy the paintings it lights, no breath to accidentally or purposely blow the flame out. I'm not content to leave it alone though. I pace the tunnel outside the cave.

Sylvan Thomson
A Portrait of the Artist as a Young Man

There was a moment, when I was about six years old, when I truly thought I was turning into a dog.

I had been playing in a stand of giant bamboo at the bottom of our garden, tearing away skirts of dried bark from the canes. The bamboo grew in interlocking segments, like fused vertebrae, and as I stood there peeling the brown bark away to expose the green skin underneath I glanced down at my hands and saw – oh, horror – a cluster of dark-brown bristles growing along my knuckles.

As a child, I spent a great deal of my time pretending to be something other than what I was, usually a dog or a boy or a fairy. When I noticed the bristles on my hand it was startling, but not particularly unexpected; after the first fright, what I mostly felt was resignation.

Standing there, solemn but reconciled, I pictured the transformation: my spine lurching forward, my face elongating into a muzzle, a tide of prickling hairs creeping up my arms until my entire body was furred and shaggy. I would drop forward on to all fours, a tail would sprout from my haunches, and from my mouth would issue not words but barks and growls.

But before that happened I had to tell my mother what was happening, tell her that she would no longer have her youngest child but instead another pet dog, a dog that would hang out in the garden with Ebony and Aslan and Cookie but would

First published on 4 October 2014 on *The Wireless*: thewireless.co.nz also always be slightly special, that would perhaps be allowed on the beds? So I ran as fast as I could to the house, up the stairs and on to the veranda where she was.

I held out my hand to show her the hairs on my knuckles, beginning a garbled explanation, but as I did so I saw that the bristles were not quite as bristly as they had been before. And when I brushed at them with my other hand they dusted off easily.

All they had been were tiny bark fibres, so fine that they had been able to embed themselves upright in my skin. Which meant I wasn't turning into a dog after all and when I realised that, I was both disappointed and relieved.

These days I think about this moment quite a lot, though now I am turning into a man, rather than a dog. And this time, I'm wholly in charge of the process.

I'm experiencing the equivalent of male puberty, brought on by a bi-weekly injection of a synthetic testosterone ester called Sustanon 250. Yet even though I have chosen to do it, it doesn't mean there aren't moments where I look at myself in the mirror, or glance down at my pale, hairy shins, and think *oh my God, what have you done to yourself?* Because there is something almost supernatural about taking testosterone.

You undergo a metamorphosis, you wake up to strange and unfamiliar things. You still look like yourself, but it's a thicker, coarser, oilier, far less pretty version of yourself.

It's not that I dislike what is happening to me; mostly I love it. Being a teenager, the second time around, is so much more fun: by this point in life you've hopefully gotten good at having sex, you can buy alcohol, do better drugs, and you no longer have to live with your parents or go to high school. With this adolescence I've learned, mostly, to leave my acne alone and I have much improved my personal style.

A lot of the time I completely forget that I didn't always look and feel like this, but then I see an old photo of myself, or catch a certain angle of my reflection in the mirror, and remember: that's right . . . I used to look like a girl. There's also part of me that still can't quite believe this process is even medically possible, that this new body and face, this funny boy who looks like me, was actually here all along, just waiting somewhere in the wings.

I know that many transgender people would say that I was always a man and that taking testosterone has just made my exterior better reflect how I felt inside, but for me that isn't true. I don't think I was ever really a *woman* but I certainly never felt like a *man*. I don't even know what I mean by *feeling like a man*, it's just a word and a set of connotations that has little to do with the many men that I know and love, but more to do with newspapers and suits, legs planted far apart, barbecue tongs, a hand clap on the back and a braying laugh. It's a word, that's all. And I am still waiting for someone to adequately explain to me what it means to be a man, or a woman – and I've asked lots of people. Nobody has any authority on anything, beyond what it means to be themselves.

For me, becoming a boy is an amazing thing; it corresponds with how I think the world should work. I've always lived half my life in the world and half my life inside books, and I feel able to move between the two easily: for instance, right now I am sitting in the Victoria University library surrounded by other diligent students tap-tapping at their keyboards. I'm hungover and I really need to pee and I'm trying to covertly see what TED Talks the girl next to me is watching, but at the same time another part of me is somewhere inside Graham Greene's scrupulous prose, accompanying a fugitive priest through a thunderstorm in 1930s Mexico.

Needless to say, I have wild expectations for the world and for my life. I want romance and adventure and unlikely heroes. I want people to have fatal flaws and dark pasts, I want there to be something in the forest, and there to always, *always* be more than meets the eye. This means that I tend to apply the standards of fiction to my life, a habit that nearly always ends in disappointment. An exception to the rule, however, seems to be transitioning. Becoming a boy for me feels like a story: like a funny, sad, joyful, cathartic coming-of-age story.

Last summer, when I had been taking testosterone for about three months, I decided that instead of flying home to Nelson for Christmas I would walk there. It would be an adventure. So I took the ferry to Picton and then set off. I went by myself and took only Jack London books and slept under the stars and washed myself in the river, half serious about this ridiculous idea of boyhood, and half laughing at myself.

On the third morning, after waking up on the bank of Pelorus River, I wandered along to the café at the DOC campground to have breakfast. It was early in the morning, no tourists awake yet, and the world was still cool and green and expectant. I could feel the day ahead of me unrolling like a spool, waiting there for me to start walking into it.

At the café I ordered eggs and coffee and sat in the window eating, my pack at my feet, feeling magnificent. When I went up to pay for the food, my Eftpos card, as it often does, declined. The brisk, middle-aged woman who had served me looked at me shrewdly over the counter, taking in my backpack and grubby, slept-in clothes. She grinned. 'Ah ha,' she said, 'a boy with no funds!' And when she said that I saw myself, suddenly, as she saw me, which for the first time was exactly how I wanted to be seen.

Testosterone has changed me physically, but it's also changed how I live in the world. There is a lightness to my life now, like someone flinging open a window in a stale room. Nothing seems to stick to me anymore. And sometimes when I'm walking into town at night, I break into a run, and start sprinting and grinning. It's like there is a wind roaring through my chest: I want to yell and dance and make out and hurl rocks into the sea and get into fights and kick things and jump off jetties.

What I'm trying to say is, life is finally living up to my expectations.

Naomi Arnold
Lost and Found

Privately, I thought the Wanderlust organisers were batty when they talked about Taupō as the country's heart chakra, a seat of powerful energy. Taupō? Taupō! Taupō was the one-street through-town on the way to somewhere else, where you stopped for an expensive pee in the Superloo and a Happy Meal at the McDonald's with the aeroplane out front which you later threw up into an ice-cream container somewhere on the Desert Road.

Later, after my parents split up, Taupō was the cold, grim shithole my dad moved to, a place of uncomfortable conversations, where the huge kauri chopping board that he had made as a young man was completely out of place; it belonged at home. I avoided Taupō, and him.

Taupō was not special. Taupō was Taupō. Wanderlust, this four-day American-born yoga and music festival that Doug and I were embarking upon, would be the first time I'd been back for years. I didn't know why they were holding it there and not somewhere more exciting. Perhaps they'd gotten a good deal on local kombucha.

As we tool past Ruapehu – we're driving up from Nelson – I go through the automated Wanderlust programme on my phone. We can study Blissology, learn about the delights of The Bhavana of Discernment, enjoy The Pleasurable Pastimes of Shiva and Shakti that Is YOU, or explore Power & Pleasure for Women: Embodying the Wild Feminine.

First published in March 2015 in *Metro* magazine: metromag.co.nz

'What do you want to do?' I ask Doug. The organisers have kindly granted us both a four-day Sage pass, and he is being polite, but can't hide his reluctance at spending Thursday to Sunday saturated in a glistering, blissful pool of what he delicately terms 'bullshit'.

'Just choose for me,' he says.

I look for the most innocuous, skipping through sessions containing red flags such as 'swami', 'yoga sutras', 'luminous', 'chakra', 'energy' and 'sacred'. There is not much left. I sign him up for the Barefoot Hike and Soul Moves and Overcoming Fear to Be Powerful and Create Your Designed Life.

'Medicinal Native Plant Hike,' I say. 'You'd like that. Ooh, look. Do you want to make your own moisturiser? Ooh. Partner Yoga. With a touch of tantra.'

'What's tantra?' he says.

'You'll like that too,' I say.

I can't really blame him for being sceptical. A divorced, lapsed Christian recovering from depression, he's spent his adult life thinking Eastern spirituality is evil and its Western devotees dippy. Bouts of anxiety still hit occasionally, like a ghost has doused him with ice water.

And here's me, in that charming way girlfriends have of eternally trying to fix their bloke, thinking he could do with a tearful, earth-shattering psychological shift, and that maybe Wanderlust could deliver it.

Anyway, I thought I could do with one myself. I am an uptight atheist with a stiff upper lip who cries secretly at sappy TV commercials. I took up yoga because a healer I once visited for a story gave me a lymphatic drainage massage and then sat me down for a talking-to.

'How much time do you spend doing nothing?' she asked.

I considered. Tried a little joke. 'Well. Reading? Folding the washing? Walking to work?'

'Those don't count,' she said.

'Well, none, I suppose,' I said, getting worried. What devastation had she felt in my glands?

'Oh, honey,' she said, 'you're on the way to getting cancer.'

Medically dubious, but definitely motivational.

There are other things bugging me. Last year, I quit my job to freelance, a move that made most people purse their lips and say, 'Ooh. You're . . . brave.' I'm also of an age where my abundantly fertile friends are on to their second and third children, and I am not. There are so many babies, in fact, that I've started visiting the Saturday Market especially to buy bulk knitted finger-puppets to parcel out as presents.

Each time they hand me one of their babies, I grip the soft little thing under her squishy armpits, look at her gummy smile and searching eyes and think, 'Why don't I want one of you?'

We are staying offsite at the Taupo Top 10 Holiday Park, so we take the Wanderbus to Wairakei Resort – and I see, as it groans closer to the thermal valley, that I am actually dead wrong about Taupō not being a place of powerful energy.

The land smokes with wrath, great curls of steam winding into the air from bush-choked gorges, cut and drained by the boiling green Waikato River. White clouds billow from culverts and grates, and I think how audacious it is for us to seal up this steaming cauldron with a skin of concrete, to pipe its boiling water for our use. It is beautiful, but it could boil you alive. I can't think how I have missed this before.

Our instructor for Partner Yoga is Israeli Hindu monk Gopala Yaffa, a tanned and smooth-skinned chap in a sleeveless

army-green shirt, with a permanent smile of contentment.
He sails up to us and puts his hand on my forearm.

'Welcome,' he says, and glides away to greet someone else.

'This is like being in church,' Doug says, a hunted look on
his face. 'The earnest stare. The smile. The forearm touch.'

'This is as far from church as you can get,' I say. 'It's basically Satanic.'

We gather on our yoga mats, which Yaffa has arranged in
a circle and which his partner, Angel, has rearranged so they
will look more beautiful in the photos. We go through a few
ice-breaking exercises of the type you do in high-school drama
class, except in high-school drama class we never rubbed each
other's shoulders while orgasmically crying out the name of
the stranger rubbing ours. (I will never forget you, Kelly.)

Next, Yaffa puts us in two circles, one inside the other, and
we face our partners. He tells us to stare into each other's eyes
and do nothing else. Just look, for a good minute.

To my horror, after a few seconds of gazing, my eyes begin
to itch and swell with tears, and Doug's eyes fill up too. Next
door, Kelly and her partner have also started crying.

'Okay,' Yaffa says, 'move to your right.' I hear a panicked
squeak and come face to face with Kelly's partner, and it
is so uncomfortable staring at her that we might as well be
naked. I vow I will overcome the shame of crying by refusing
to look away from her, but she cannot hold my gaze and keeps
glancing away, sniffing and giggling in embarrassment.

It's awful. But it goes on. We move to our right again, and a
handsome lad in his twenties turns up and holds me in his eyes.
He is tall and lean with broad shoulders, and I feel ripped
open, all my shame, my pettiness on display – my insecuri-
ties, jealousies, lies, the coins I nicked from my mother's purse,
the time I stole my nana's chocolate Easter bunny, the time I

whacked my dog, that I think he is gorgeous, that I know he knows I think it.

My cheeks burn. He can see all this and I am stripped bare and can't stand it, but the torture goes on and on with different people until Yaffa tells us to stop and hug the person in front of us, and he is kind enough to have carefully orchestrated it so we are in front of our partners.

I cling to Doug like someone drowning.

Next we have to close our eyes, walk among the group and gently feel for our partner's face in the dark.

'I knew it was you,' Doug says when he finds me. 'I knew straight away by the texture of your skin.' By the time we've done body-balancing poses and given each other a Thai massage and closed our eyes and opened our mouths like baby birds while Yaffa places a piece of organic vegan chocolate on our tongues, we have fallen into the weekend, and who we were before seems very far away.

We spend Thursday on separate schedules, moving between yoga, talks and meditation, and I meet Wanderlust's target market in the flesh. From what I can see and hear, their ethnicity and place of origin vary, though I know the stats say they have an average age of 33 and are 85 per cent female.

They've got bored with the binge-drinking New Years and the summer rock festivals. They love the outdoors. They love to dance. Most of their clothes carry at least one small silver stamp of Lululemon on their lower backs or between their shoulder blades.

This describes me exactly, and I have the unsettling thought that I am not a special and unique flower but am instead absolutely ordinary, our pants from the same factory line, the little shards thrown at us by life all roughly interchangeable, though they haven't derailed us so much that we can't spend hundreds of dollars on yoga classes, accommodation, travel and a ticket.

I spy on a few classes, and watch some of the women arching through their poses. One has painted her nails to match her yoga pants, which are mottled like a swirly pastel ice-cream. In the late afternoon, there's a welcome event with drinks, and I notice that someone has already come up with my novelty yoga t-shirt idea, I'M HERE FOR THE SAVASANA, which is disappointing, but there is free sangria to drink.

One woman is wearing what amounts to a bikini and is dancing alone in front of the stage, tossing around a messy head of hair. She is smoking, which I think rather daring – and admirable – at a wellness festival, and she returns for cup after cup of sangria. A festival volunteer hovers as I pause at the rubbish bins to drop off my own drained vessel.

'Oh, that's compostable!' she says, and takes it from me.

I keep seeing that guy from Partner Yoga around, and every time I do I feel naked again and filled with shame. I try to avoid him. That evening, after what must have been a particularly powerful lesson on self-limiting core beliefs from New Zealander Jase Te Patu, Doug requests space, and I circle about him warily, not sure what he is thinking and too afraid to ask.

The next day, I go alone to a 6.30 a.m. chakra cleanse with Aucklander Denise Ferguson. I had never before thought my chakras were particularly dirty, but for the sake of research I am willing to give them a good polish.

I join dozens of others at a blue-tented spot on the edge of the resort called The Quiet Place, and close my eyes. As Ferguson moves us through our bodies, I start to feel the air funnelling through my nose, and the persistent nudge of my heartbeat. Hey, it says, and I think of the push and flow of blood. Hey. Hey. Hey. Hey. You can breathe. You're alive. Suddenly, I can't believe my luck.

Towards the end, Ferguson tells us to imagine the future, which is also now and also the past, or something, and I see a quiet, dark-green garden shed at home, which we don't have, but it is like the one my grandparents had when they were alive, with seedlings potted in egg cartons on the white windowsill.

Then my eye shifts to the right, to the north, where the sun is coming in the doorway, and I see a blonde girl of about five standing there, silhouetted against the light. The girl is me and yet is not me, because she is wearing a dress that my mother could never have gotten me into without a fistfight.

She is looking at me with her right hand on the doorframe, and her left toe lifts to scratch her calf, and I remember I have seen her before, visiting my head, years ago, though I don't recall when, and had forgotten about her until right now in this valley of steam and eucalypts. It is such a powerful jolt that tears spring forth again, which is really annoying.

Because: a child. Really fucking subtle, subconscious. And, oh, she's asking to come in! To enter a place we have yet to build, but that I have paced out on our hillside and sat in its square with my dog and looked out across the valley at the seagulls wheeling in the summer evening thermals! That's so fucking deep!

And, oh – wait. She was standing in the north door. And what is Wanderlust's slogan, which I've been reading on email after email for six months? Find your true north. Oh, shit. I am getting old. I am becoming a cliché. Worse. I am becoming *Eat, Pray, Love*.

I don't know where you start and finish with stuff like this. When do these visions or wants or heartfelt desires become something you need to pay attention to and act upon, and when are you just being a self-indulgent dickhead? I have to open my eyes to see how the others are coping – maybe they're all gathered in a circle laughing, and I am the butt of a huge joke, with my thoughts playing out on a screen strung across the front of the tent.

I sneak a peek. All is calm. Everyone is cocooned in their private realm like astronauts in sleep pods, crossing the universe in ageless slumber. In fact, I am quite pleased to see the girl next to me has fresh wet cheeks. Good.

Because I know the biochemistry of meditation. I know there is a rational biological explanation for the visions visited upon you during it, as well as just before you fall asleep, and when you dream, and in the last images before death.

And after my day at Wanderlust yesterday, I know I should be only witnessing my thoughts and letting them ripple across my mind, not dragging them under the surface to fight them. I know all this, but still. I am undone. I have seen that little girl before.

Friday afternoon. Doug and I haven't seen each other all day, and when we do, he is being especially weird. Throughout his depression, I have gotten used to him acting oddly, but he's always sought me out.

We are used to telling each other everything, but here I am lying on my back on the seat of a picnic table in the holiday park, my foot bouncing the concrete, my right hand up to block the glare of the setting summer sun, and I am waiting for him to break up with me.

He is in the kitchen. He's been sitting there for half an hour;

in fact, after our quite intense start at Partner Yoga, he has been avoiding me for most of the time we've been here, looking guilty.

If he isn't working up the courage to shatter our three years together, he's playing his friend Glen at Scrabble on his phone.

I am meant to be cooking dinner out on the barbecue, but I'm too full for that now, because instead of charring the lamb and warm vegetable salad I thought we'd eat happily for dinner, I have slotted Weet-Bix after Weet-Bix into an aluminium mug, poured milk over them and eaten them, glowering at the happy couples walking past. I binge on Weet-Bix. I get to seven before I groan and flop over on the seat.

I lie here and obsess over the awkward conversation to come, the lists, the spreadsheets. I will leave the country, I think. I could go to Dubai and work. I never did sort out who put how much money into the house. Guess I won't be seeing his kids again. Oh my God – who gets the dog?

I don't know how we went from reasonably happy to this in just two days, and why I am feeling like such a moody teenager, but I lay the blame squarely on Wanderlust. I had thought he would question some of his assumptions about the shape he's made of the world and his place in it, but I did not think he would start questioning us.

He emerges, looking guilty again, and starts to slice an avocado. I put the lamb on the barbecue. I have vowed to say nothing, but will wait until he comes out with whatever is bugging him, like a supportive girlfriend. I point out the cute little kitten that is winding its way around the ankles of the happy campers.

'It looks like a stray,' he says. 'Look at its flanks. It's starving.'

I will say nothing.

That night, he is in a tangle over all the crud Wanderlust is bringing up – about his past, what he thinks of himself, his future, his god, his family hurts, his childhood pain, his revelation that what happens to these devotees is just like what happens at church: the tears, the endorphins, the community, the healing – all of which somehow reinforces religion and yet undermines it, too.

'This is all familiar,' he says. 'People carrying around their yoga mats like Bibles.'

'Like prayer mats,' I say, but he hasn't mentioned us, and I am saying nothing, so I start a meditation app that one of the speakers has recommended, and it quickly drops us into sleep.

Once, when I was a child, my father and I paddled a kayak out on to Lake Taupō. He was not given to coddling children; as a horse-mad eleven-year-old, I had seen in the paper that a girl with leukaemia had gotten a pony from the Make-A-Wish Foundation. Damn, I thought. Lucky her.

'Dad,' I said. 'If I got leukaemia, would you get me a pony?'

'No,' he said.

Floating on the surface of the lake, he told me that beneath the lapping blue, the ducks and the tangling weeds that gave you shivers when they brushed your legs, there was the secret heart of a volcano and rivers of hot magma that once built to the biggest eruption the world had ever seen, which blew out the centre of the country.

Enormous scales of rock were still now sliding across each other, forming an immense chain of burp and murmur that crossed landscapes too vast for me to comprehend – from Ruapehu and Ngauruhoe to the blasted top of Tarawera, Rotorua, and out into the Pacific.

'Rivers of boiling rock,' he said, as we bobbed. 'Right down beneath this kayak. So hot they would melt your foot right off if you stepped in them.'

'What would happen if it erupted now?' I asked him.

'We'd live for about five seconds,' he said, with relish. 'Probably less. We'd burn alive, and nothing would be left.'

That kind of thing leaves an impression on a kid. I was transfixed, staring down into the deep blue. I worried about our cats, Sooty and Pumpkin, who I imagined would survive the eruption but would be left alone to prowl the ash pan left behind, and would probably have to tear the last remnants of flesh from our scorched bones to survive. At least, Sooty would, the shithead.

'Couldn't we run anywhere?'

'No time!' he said, describing Ruapehu's acidic crater lake, the lahars.

'Is it going to happen when we are alive?' I asked.

'Well, it's overdue,' he said.

The next morning is better. Doug seems more relaxed and I am convinced the meditation is helping.

'Look what Forbes says. It's just as powerful as medication,' I say, bringing up articles and studies on my phone. 'And no side effects.' He just nods.

I go to a healing circle, and later, when we meet for a lunch of raw falafel wraps and dairy-free coconut ice-blocks, the gorgeous man from Partner Yoga comes up to say hi. It turns out that Doug has befriended him. I stand there blushing furiously as they exchange chat about acro-yoga. His name is Josh and he is a visitor from Hawke's Bay.

I want to shout 'I'M IN LOVE WITH YOU!' but he goes off to his next class. As we start to leave the lawn, a woman comes up to me and says, 'Naomi?'

It is a girl from my school. She is a year younger than me and has three kids, all of whom are cartwheeling around the grass right now. She can't be old enough to have three children. We chat for a bit about the festival. I explain that I have been crying a lot because of these damn classes. She says she has come just for the day. Soon it becomes obvious I have no idea who she is.

'You don't remember me, do you?' she says. 'I've changed a lot since then. But you look exactly the same.'

It's my damn ponytail, and my clothes. It's really time I got a hairstyle and some sort of fashion sense. But look, I whisper to Doug after she leaves. She is a year younger than me, and she has three children. Aren't they gorgeous?

He puts his arm around me. 'Do you want kids?' he asks, for what must be the hundredth time.

'I don't know,' I say, for what must be the thousandth.

That evening, we have some time to kill before the concert – Xavier Rudd and Nightmares on Wax – and I haven't managed to go on any of the bushwalk tours, so we set off down a lane of eucalypts towards the Waikato River, where there is a hot spring on the shore.

Along the way, Doug tells me about his Medicinal Native Plant Hike, and picks off the young shoots of the hangihangi and gives them to me to eat. They taste like peas. He points out the native fuchsia, telling me that the healer said it was used to cure female ills, and the tōtara, for male troubles.

At the hot spring, we strip off and sit in the thermal bath, the stones burning our feet. Light rain falls, dappling the surface of the river, already pockmarked from where geothermal bubbles are breaking the surface. I sweep more hot water from the next pool into ours. It burns; it must be close to 60 degrees.

It is a magical spot, and I realise I haven't really been fair to Taupō, and the whole place is beautiful and my parents' divorce and my dad's pain and the kauri chopping board in the wrong house have poisoned it in my mind, like the faint scent of sulphur that occasionally wreathes the breath of the wind.

I recall that I now have that chopping board at home. Maybe I should have brought it here, and burned it, or something.

I confess to Doug that I have a crush on the young man in Partner Yoga.

'I knew it,' he says.

I confess that I thought he was going to break up with me.

'That's the last thing I want,' he says. 'Who else would put up with me?'

'No one,' I say.

'And who else would put up with you?'

He says he just wants to work things out by himself. That Wanderlust has given him time to think. That the talks and classes have unlocked something that has been stuck for a long time. That I should shut up sometimes. That he prayed again, and it wasn't really Eastern or Western but he did it, for the first time in ages.

I begin to hope the ice-water ghost has buggered off. It's not the first time I've hoped that, and it won't be the last, but it is nice to sit in the hot pool for a bit and think what that would be like, anyway. Time to go home, and get him to build that shed. Oh right. I should shut up sometimes.

'What were you doing in the kitchen the other night?' I ask.

'Playing Scrabble,' he says.

Above the pool, where the underground heat warms the air, wild blackberries are ripening more quickly than those around them. Some of them are ripe already.

I pick off a few, and eat them.

Dan Eichblatt
On Being a Gayby Daddy

I'm shivering in my driveway, clutching a small plastic cup wrapped in kitchen towel. In the cup – fresh semen. Don't be alarmed, it's my own. In the approaching car are my friends Jane and Melissa. They pull to a stop, I hand it through the window, we grin. Jane tucks the package in her cleavage. They do a 180 and speed off to beat the rush-hour traffic.

And thus, the miracle of life.

How did we get here? A 35-year-old gay man and his gay girl chums, Doing Procreation like a dodgy drug deal in a suburban cul-de-sac? The answer, like most things in life, is more straightforward than some may have you believe.

It's a familiar refrain for many gay men. 'If we're single when we're (x age), we should definitely just have a kid together.' Over casks of Miami wine cooler and cheap clove cigarettes (the 1990s, you have much to answer for) we would jokingly plan our presumably barren futures with girlfriends we knew would never lack male attention. Their futures, we were certain, were secure. We had seen it in films, heard it in songs. Our parents were living proof of the heterosexual ideal; our more confident friends were grappling with its challenges already.

Our own futures? These were less certain, having few visible role models to which to aspire, and fewer (if that's possible) positive examples of gay romantic relationships. Television and films in the 1980s did not fill us with much hope – exaggerated

First published on 31 July 2014 in *Impolitikal*: impolitikal.com camp 'nelly' characters were sexless, two-dimensional and side-lined, reduced to catty one-liners and arched eyebrows, forever alone. 'I am free', indeed. At the other end of the spectrum, the exaggerated 'masculine' representations of gay men were furtive, silent and predatory, inhabiting an aggressively sexual shadow world of bars, parks and alleyways. Cruising and *Cruising*. It was sex – the more anonymous the better – not love they were after. Between the two stood the beige, sweater-vested urban gay, de-sexed and entirely unthreatening. He was a placeholder, used by female characters to express their feelings before a 'real man' could take his place. He was reassuring, comforting and utterly boring.

I grew up in a world that, culturally, didn't really acknowledge my existence. Perhaps that's just how teenagers feel. I was a good student and a pretty well-behaved son. I had great friends, played in bands, acted in plays and had jobs from a young age. While never naturally sporty, I was fit and active enough. I was also sarcastic and argumentative and judgemental, especially of the effortlessly 'cool' kids. I wore different coloured Converse on each foot because . . . actually, I forget why. I wore t-shirts emblazoned with indie band logos handed down from my much cooler older sister, Sam. Thankfully, no one asked me about these bands; the boy with a bedroom wallpapered in Kylie posters would have probably stuttered 'Oh, them . . . they're, like, really alternative . . . and stuff.' Small mercies.

Occasionally I would be called a 'faggot' or 'poof' by kids at school. 'Faggot' is an ugly, brutal word. It crushes and diminishes and dismisses in one whipcrack. That final 't' stings like venom.

I found 'poof' worse, though. The word was too knowing. It seemed to casually flay me open and expose a truth I'd desperately tried to hide from myself. That *thing*. I had bargained with God to make it *not true*. Now, it seemed, everyone knew. I was just a poof, and nothing more.

My friend Jane was cooler than me. We first met when we were eleven or twelve, spent our formative years getting suburban drunk together, and spent a good part of our twenties together in London. At high school, she played piano better than me, seemed more confident, and had a steady stream of boyfriends. While I fumbled embarrassingly in romantic ('romantic') overtures to the opposite sex, everyone around me appeared to be revelling in athletic, frequent and successful bouts of Fucking. I was Richie Cunningham stranded in the *Red Shoe Diaries*, with a crap '90s soundtrack to boot.

I came out to my sister shortly before my twentieth birthday, my mum the day after my birthday, and my dad three days after that. Instead of a seismic catastrophe, the revelation was rather a damp squib. My sister was thrilled I'd finally figured out what she'd known for years, and we celebrated with cheap tequila. Mum was surprised, surprisingly (I'd dressed up as Madonna for my fourteenth birthday party, after all) and my dad said he didn't really concern himself with who I went to bed with as long as I was happy and healthy. Textbook example of a Good Coming Out – cheers, family!

Jane had a different route to her eventual happiness with Melissa, but by our early thirties we were reasonably, relatively sorted. I became a high-school teacher, Jane was in IT and Melissa a lawyer. I had met a lovely man, a graphic designer, and was enjoying my first proper, adult relationship.

It was New Year's Eve 2012 when the idea came up as more than a drunken musing. Would I be willing to help these two secure, happy and loving women reach their dream of motherhood? Like, for real this time.

I had long entertained the thought of being a dad. As a teenager, I simply assumed it would happen at some point. Coming out didn't change that too much, although the path to fatherhood would be different. But by my thirties, the desire to be a father had faded. I had two beautiful godchildren and plenty of friends with kids. I worked with hundreds of teenagers each year. Half of my Facebook friends had, alarmingly and disconcertingly, replaced their profile pictures with images of their gurgling offspring, and I knew more about leaky nipples and the variety of effluvia babies make than I would ever care to. Children's birthday parties gave me anxiety.

However, that primal tug (what would it look like? what would it *be* like?) reawakened with this proposition. Minimal responsibility or effort, for something that would make my friends happy. I honestly didn't think it much further through.

And it was so easy! After I got myself all checked out by a doctor, it was just me and my little cup, waiting for the day. I was alerted by a nervous text message ('we're on our way'), did the business and handed over the package. I imagine the insemination ceremony featured incantations, candles and complicated pulley systems, if the 'moral' 'majority' (sic) are to be believed. Pentagrams and animal sacrifice. Offerings to Sappho and Diana. The usual.

It didn't work that first time and I suffered a brief but crushing and completely ridiculous sense of failure. I chastised my stupid gay sperm. They were clearly confused, too many years getting happy and dancing to the Vengaboys to know a ripe egg when they saw it. Probably thought it was a disco ball. Or a handbag to dance around.

We tried again the following month. By this time I had come to my senses and understood that it might take a while. That month between attempts had given us all time for reflection.

Naturally, we had considered the implications for the child. How could we not? A child with two mothers will have questions about its genesis. A child with two mothers may be seen by others as different. Strange. Even blasphemous. External forces, beyond the control or influence of its loving home and extended family, may undermine its sense of worth. The world can be a brutal, unforgiving enough place without the added pressures of a slightly unconventional family structure to explain.

It's been said before by far cleverer people than me, but children only know what they are taught. Hateful or judgemental attitudes are fostered, or quashed, by adults. Should my friends cede their desire for a family to strangers who can barely stomach the existence of gay people? Should an innocent child shoulder this unasked-for burden? A child is not a political tool of subversion, an example or a symbol. The queer activist inside me wrestled with the beauty and simplicity of procreation and family.

These thoughts, and many more, crowded my mind alongside more prosaic musings. What would the child call me? How would I refer to him or her? The words 'father', 'son/daughter', 'parent' stretched and twisted and remained unsatisfying. Language, my faithful ally, had not made provisions. What would happen in a tragedy? How much say, if any, would I have in its upbringing? Church or no church? When is the right time to have The Talk? Will anyone expect me to discuss these 'birds and bees' if there are two birds and the bee has a boyfriend?

The second attempt, astonishingly, worked. Melissa was righteously up the duff. Knocked up. The bun was in the oven. She was beatifically With Child. We had made a gayby.

Theo was born in early December, 2013. He's pretty goddamn adorable too. He smiles a lot. He is in great health.

Jane and Melissa are utterly smitten. He is wanted. I am, for the sake of ease, his godfather. He will be told about his conception when the time is right. He has aunties and uncles and cousins aplenty. My mum and dad are grandparents, of a kind, and have become quite besotted. The kid is loved.

Jane, Melissa and little Theo are a regular family. Two committed women raising an undoubtedly open-minded little boy. They will face regular challenges and overcome them together as best they can, as all families do. The naysayers who mindlessly crow that all children need a father unwittingly judge *all* women who raise children without a present male. I wonder if they understand how complicit they are in perpetuating damage, blinded as they are by their moral hubris. I will be present, as much as I can be. Jane's older brothers and father too. Friends and teachers and extended family members. It takes a village, right?

I think back to the 1990s and our restless uncertainty about the future. Our drunken prophecies and semi-serious plans and first kisses and no road maps. The fear of falling and the eventual, startling gratitude that we did. Where would we be, what would we do? We hoped the world would make some room for us. We hoped our lives would mean something. There is no ending to this story, no guarantee that everything will be fine, no reassurance that It Gets Better. But it can, and it might, and it did for me.

Steve Braunias
Man on Fire

It was a winter's evening last July at about six, just gone dark, and I should have lit the fire. It was a cold night. But perhaps I had lit the fire, because all of a sudden there was the sharp smell of smoke.

I was sitting next to my seven-year-old daughter on the blue couch in the lounge. My fiancée had gone out for a brisk walk around the block. The two of us stayed indoors, lazy and companionable, to watch a really good episode of Disney comedy series *Good Luck Charlie*.

It's about the Duncan family of Denver. Bob is a bug exterminator, and his wife Amy is a frustrated actress. They have five kids. The gorgeous Bridgit Mendler plays the eldest daughter, Teddy, who films video diaries of their crazy life.

Sometimes I wish our lives had a laugh track, like on *Good Luck Charlie*. A studio audience would be on hand to hoot at our brilliant and improvised dialogue, the things we say around the dinner table, at bath time, on the couch.

I said to my daughter, 'Can you smell something?'

She said, 'Huh?'

We were sitting directly opposite the fireplace. I got up and examined the fireplace. Smoke wasn't coming from the fireplace, on account of the fact it hadn't been lit.

I rushed to the kitchen. The oven wasn't on and neither were

First published in the *New Zealand Herald*'s *Canvas* magazine on
21 February 2015.

any of the elements, or the toaster, or the kettle. The smell was now very bad, and I was suddenly afraid.

Our house is designed for upstairs living; I rushed downstairs, on a kind of whim. I supposed the smoke was coming up from the garage, or the fusebox in the laundry, or the electric heater in my carpeted office – that heater had once singed my overcoat. I still wore that overcoat. I couldn't bear to part with it. Like all nervous wrecks, I am attached to old familiar objects; they work like a compass, they tell you where you are.

There was no fire downstairs, no smoke. I rushed back upstairs and there was smoke, thick and black and rolling in like a storm, in the hallway. I turned on the hallway lights. They didn't work. I couldn't see anything. I realised later that the lights were working, but the smoke had blacked them out.

I rushed down the hallway in search of the fire. It wasn't in the bathroom. It wasn't in the spare room. It wasn't in our bedroom. There was one room left to rush into: the fire was in our daughter's bedroom. I stared at the flames. They were nearly beautiful, definitely very pretty.

A few months later, I read *Young Men and Fire*, a terrifying book by Norman Maclean, which recreates the tragedy of fifteen firefighters who were killed in a forest fire in Montana in 1949. Maclean had worked on fire crews. He knew about fires, about the speed of their apocalypse. He described the beginning of one insane blaze: 'At first it was no bigger than a small campfire, looking more like something you could move up close to and warm your hands against, than something that in a few minutes could leave your remains lying with nothing but a belt.'

The flames in our daughter's bedroom were bright yellow and blood red. I think I saw orange, too. The carpet was on fire, next to her bed, beside the oil heater. The flames were not quite knee height. The rest of the room was in darkness.

I rushed back to the kitchen and put a pot in the sink and turned on the tap. The water flowed at its usually languid pace. I yelled, 'Where are you?'

She yelled, 'Downstairs!'

I yelled, 'Good girl!'

The pot had gathered maybe four or five inches of water. That would do. I rushed back down the hallway, and for a moment, I was lost, didn't know where I was. The smoke had got darker, thicker. It was complete, you couldn't see anything except smoke. My eyes watered and it felt as though I was being strangled, I staggered into our daughter's bedroom and threw the pot of water on the pretty fire.

It went out.

*

I did everything wrong. But the things I did do weren't as bad or stupid and dangerous as the things I didn't do. I didn't take my daughter and evacuate the premises. I didn't call 111. I didn't even have smoke alarms. In fact, I'd taken them out. They were such a nuisance. I hated their pathetic wailings every time they responded to the slightest puff of smoke from a toaster.

I shouldn't have tried to put the fire out. It seemed like an important priority at the time. I was scared and in a state of panic and I rushed around like a fool, downstairs and upstairs, poking my nose into all the wrong rooms, but I had a job to do and actually I remained calm deep inside. No fears for steady men. The interruption to *Good Luck Charlie* and the threat to home and life was something that called for action. The thing to do was find the fire and deal to it.

God only knows how I failed to electrocute myself when I threw water over the flames and the heater. It must have just missed the electrical circuits. And what was I thinking when

I then calmly unplugged the heater? Whenever someone asks that question – what were you thinking? – the answer is always the same. You weren't thinking.

I took the heater downstairs, and tossed the wretched thing into the back yard. I opened all the windows. My fiancée returned from her walk, and saw enormous gusts of smoke pouring out of the house. 'Everything's perfectly all right,' I said.

Our daughter was thrilled. She had been very active. She said later that after she yelled out that she was downstairs, she got it into her head that she should call the fire service, so she raced back up the stairs for the phone – she also wanted to call her mum. She got as far as the top of the stairs, and the smoke drove her out.

There was a fish tank with two goldfish in our daughter's room. I carried it downstairs. After I started wiping down the walls with a broom and a wet cloth, I got it into my head that I should call the fire service. I apologised to the man for bothering him, and explained there had been a small fire, which I'd put out, but wondered if they might like to come over and check to see if things were safe.

'Christ,' he said. 'We're leaving now.'

'Well,' I said, 'there's certainly no need for sirens or any of that drama.'

He'd already hung up.

The sirens bellowed as the truck turned into our street. Men in helmets tromped up the stairs and inspected the property and declared it was safe. They inspected the oil heater and declared it was faulty. The thing had melted, caught fire.

They said we were lucky. They said another thirty seconds in the smoke in the hallway or my daughter's bedroom and I would have been killed. They said something about carbon monoxide but I didn't really listen to the details.

One of them said, 'You look a bit rough.'

I said, 'No, I don't.'

He called an ambulance. They said we all had to go to hospital. Our daughter was ecstatic. Her good humour and intense curiousity wore off after a few hours of tests and waiting for results of tests. She and her mum got the all-clear at about 10 p.m., and went to my fiancée's parents' house for the night. Because I'd inhaled a lot of smoke, I was asked to stay for further tests.

I got sick of sitting around with a needle taped to my arm so I fled at about midnight. I went home. The house was freezing. The goldfish swam very low in the fish tank. The cats were hungry. I shut myself in the lounge and tried to sleep on the couch. I couldn't sleep. I kept thinking of how I had failed my family, that I hadn't got my daughter out of the house; and I also thought about what might have happened to her if the fire had started a few hours later, when she lay fastened with sleep in her bed, next to the oil heater.

From Norman Maclean's book, imagining how the fifteen firefighters perished in Montana: 'They did not die of burning. The burning came afterwards . . . Heat and loneliness became the only remaining properties . . . . The heat even burned out fear . . . . You sink back into the region of strange gases where there is no oxygen and here you die in your lungs; then you sink into the fire that consumes.'

But we had survived. The house had survived. We were like the Duncan family of Denver in *Good Luck Charlie*: we had experienced adversity, but came to no harm. The man from the insurance company arrived the next day, and set to work. It took a week for the cleaners to finish the job. I slept badly, and was frightened and ashamed and tearful, but a bit of mild trauma never hurt anyone.

I got a call from my quack to come in and discuss the results of the boring tests at hospital. I made an appointment. He said my heartbeat was a bit irregular.

'Oh well,' I said.

'There's something else,' he said.

I looked at him.

'They found a shadow on your lungs,' he said.

It was 24 millimetres in density and it might be cancer.

It wasn't my house that caught fire. It was me. I was on fire.

*

Burning man, struck dumb – what to do, how to respond? I have long been preoccupied with the fairly humourless and probably Darwinian notion that life is a test. It tests your decisions, your nerve, your character, everything. The fire was a test. I kind of passed – I was the hero who saved the house from burning down. I kind of failed – I was the blunderer who risked his daughter's life. I wasn't up to the test of cancer. I gave in straight away, admitted defeat.

I paid the appointment fee in silence. The receptionist looked away. I felt as weightless as smoke, and drifted across the road. I have always loathed the idea of bucket lists; they're grandiose, self-serving, predictable. It occurred to me that one thing I'd always wanted to do was take the bus to the shops in Glen Eden.

You never hear anyone talk about that obscure suburb in West Auckland, but I've always liked the look of it. It feels like a town on a volcanic plateau, somewhere remote, windswept. It feels deeply New Zealand – it feels old and familiar, and I wanted to cling to it like a favourite old overcoat.

A railroad passes through it. When the trains approach, bells ring, and there is a drone like a vuvuzela. The railway platform is at the top of a gentle slope, and looks over the main shopping street. Towering over the shops is a large billboard of barrister Greg Presland's face. He looks like he might be Glen Eden's hanging judge.

I had a cup of tea and a toasted sandwich at the Trocadero tea-room, and bought a book about the Lockerbie air disaster at BE second-hand books. I mooched around. I was stunned, speechless, very tired. I was in hell. I waited for a train. A tough old broad sat next to me on the platform and started complaining that her partner had given her a black eye, and wouldn't share his cans of alcohol. She pointed him out – a shambling figure drinking in the bushes.

Then she said, 'Come with me to the toilet.'

I said, 'No, I'm good, thanks.'

She said, 'Let's have some fun.'

I said, 'I'm sick. Leave me alone.'

Was I sick? I broke the news at home that night. 'It might be nothing,' I said.

I went to hospital for a CT scan. They said the results would come through in about a week. The days limped by. I focused on work. I interviewed a nice man called Andy Stankovich, a singer who was preparing to stage an Elvis tribute at the Civic Theatre. I wanted to say to him, 'Help me, Elvis.'

Our daughter went very quiet. She asked questions about my health when I wasn't there. She stayed close when I was there. We were lying on top of the bed one day after school when the phone rang. I picked it up. It wasn't a long conversation. I put the phone down, and she said, 'What's wrong?'

I had just been told that I was out of work. My position at *Metro* magazine was being 'disestablished'.

At least it took my mind off dying. Was I dying? 'We'll get through this,' my fiancée said. I was on fire, but I was lucky. I had love. We clung to each other. I felt I was disappearing from view. I've never much cared for myself, but I couldn't bear the thought of abandoning my family.

The hospital called. The results would be with my doctor in two days' time, a Wednesday. I interviewed Andy Stankovich again. He walked around his house singing to himself, 'It's now or never . . .'

It rained very hard and was bitterly cold on Wednesday. I went to *Metro* in the morning for the last time to listen to some HR bore talk about redundancy calculations. The doctor's appointment was in the afternoon.

There were four workmen on the motorway wearing gas masks and protective orange suits.

We parked in the supermarket car park next to the doctor's surgery, and there was a busker dressed all in black with a Texan tie. He sounded like he was playing a death ballad.

We held hands and waited in reception. The doctor stepped out of his office. He looked very grave. He didn't say anything; he beckoned me with his finger.

There were two glass paperweights on his desk. I could see over to the North Shore though his window. The sky was white. He made small talk, and he didn't look me in the eye. Obviously he was about to give me bad news. But then he gave a slow smile, and said, 'We're winning.'

It wasn't cancer. It was nothing, merely the presence of smoke from the fire. It had collapsed the lung, but only temporarily. I didn't know how thoroughly depressed I had been until I heard the good news, and was finally, for the first time in a long while, happy. I was safe. My family were safe. The fire was out. At last, for good. For now, till next time. Life is a test, and the tests never end.

Lynn Jenner
The Ring Story

Christchurch, 29 April 2011

Of course, there are rumours that there has been much more looting in the Red Zone than is being officially admitted, the lawyer in Christchurch said when I phoned him about my mother's diamond ring, worth as much as a new European car, and last seen in a jeweller's shop in Cashel Mall five days before the earthquake.

Then there was a silence.

There are rumours that it is the soldiers, he said.

Another silence.

There's such a lot of property in there at the moment and no one really knows who owns it, he said. Most people have turned out to be very honest, he said. But some haven't.

Realistically, I said, what do you think the chances are that my mother will get her ring back?

Nil, he said. You should make an insurance claim.

Sooo, I said, feeling free to speculate now that we had received our advice, what's to stop the jeweller from keeping the ring, not telling his insurance company he has it, and selling the stone in Amsterdam?

Nothing, the lawyer said. I think you should make a claim.

First published in Lynn's book *Lost and Gone Away* (Auckland University Press) in July 2015.

He didn't respond at all to my next suggestion that we could perhaps retain a member of a motorcycle gang to shake down the jeweller on our behalf.

After a long silence he said, let me know if you have any trouble with the insurance company.

*

Sometime in the 1980s my mother had inherited this ring.

A canny Scottish farming woman, doing very well, thank you, was the first owner of the ring. She was a big woman with strong hands. *She* wore the ring to church on Christmas Day and when she went to the races.

She kept the ring wrapped in cotton wool, in a round ivory box with a carved lid inside her wooden jewellery box on her dressing table which had been brought out from Scotland. Huge dark and shiny furniture. Carved edges. Solid brass handles. When she died, at the end of a good long life, she left the ring, along with her maiden name, to her daughter, who, when she died, left the ring to my mother. The huge dark furniture and the Highland flower name went somewhere else.

Himself, as the farming woman called her husband, had inherited one farm, and then he had four, and although he grumbled about the wharfies and their revolutionary tendencies and the effect of wage increases on the cost of shipping, over the years he made pretty fair prices on his mutton and wool. In his fifties he became ill with a disease that caused unbearable pain. A long sea voyage was prescribed. That and morphine. Knowing he would never work again, he gave the farms to his sons, who lost them almost immediately.

My mother wasn't the sort of woman to go to church on Christmas Day or to the races, but for the sake of a farmer's wife from Palmerston and a Highland flower name, which had by then been lost in a sea of men's names, she would sometimes wear the ring. Mostly the ring lived in the ivory box with the carved lid, inside her plain modern jewellery box on her plain modern dressing table, its value something of a worry.

With my father lying beside her in bed, big and warm like a bear, she didn't worry too much. But after he died she took the ring into town and, with a certain amount of formality, placed it in a safe deposit box at the Westpac Bank and there it stayed, in a cool dark box, for a decade or so. Late in 2010 my mother received a letter from her insurance company, saying that the valuation on her ring was out of date. The value of precious stones and gold had been rising rapidly, the letter said, and she should have the ring revalued. What a waste of money having insurance, we said. Surely items in a safe deposit box in the vault of a bank could never be stolen. We thought this was quite funny. We did not consider that the building itself might become a pile of rubble.

My mother decided she should follow the advice of the insurance company and get the ring revalued, but there was a problem. Over the years she had lost the key to the safe deposit box. Some months went by, during which we turned out every corner of her drawers and looked for the key to the safe deposit box, but we never found it. We did find a number of keys for which we could find no locks, but that was no help.

17 February 2011

My mother paid a locksmith to come to the bank, had a new key made for the safe deposit box, opened it, took out the ring in its ivory box and put the box in her purse. Then she

walked down a couple of streets to the jeweller in Cashel
Mall. I'm not sure why she took the ring to this particular
jeweller.

22 February 2011: Earthquake Day

Our main concern was her, but her main concern was her
house, her cat, and the fact that there was no power, water or
sewerage. I don't know when she first remembered the ring –
it might have been after a few days. It is also possible that she
remembered straight away and spoke about it, but for a few
days I wasn't listening.

I do remember that we talked about it a few times during
March. She would use a pragmatic tone. Oh yes, she would say,
the ring is almost certainly gone, but it doesn't matter really.
People have had such terrible things happen to them. Then we
would discuss those terrible things.

As time went by our discussions changed a little. We would
each say that the ring was lost. I would say it was lost in the
same way as I might refer to the scent of honeysuckle in an
English country garden before World War I. She would say the
ring was *probably* lost. It took me a few weeks to notice this
difference, more time to realise that the person who should
do something was me, and more time again to actually do
anything.

In the meantime I attended a poetry reading at which a
woman collapsed, took out a new mortgage and read books
about sculptural representations of the Holocaust.

19 March 2011

I phoned the jeweller's shop in Cashel Mall. There was no
reply. I pictured the phone ringing in the Red Zone. Perhaps
there were other phones ringing? There was an email address

in the jeweller's advertisement in the Yellow Pages, so I sent an email.

Hello

I don't know how things are with your people and your business – I hope you are all alive and unhurt, and that you might be reading emails. My mother had a diamond ring in being valued on Feb 22. She has asked me to enquire about the ring. We assume it would be in your safe and that you can't access it. Could you please help us with any information on the ring? It isn't as important as people, but it is of sentimental as well as financial value to my mother who is in her eighties. It would be great to hear from you

Lynn

My email came back to me with a message saying the jeweller's inbox was full.

31 *March 2011*
My mother read an article in the *Listener* about frustrated businessmen who were unable to get in to their businesses in the Red Zone because Civil Defence authorities wouldn't give permission. Gerald (his real name), a jewellery valuer, also from Cashel Mall, was quoted. He found it hard to understand some business people taking a passive attitude, moaning about not being able to get in to their businesses, and meanwhile he had been in to his business three times, he said. My mother thought Gerald might know something about the ring situation because his shop was near the jeweller. I thought that idea was a bit far-fetched, but said I'd try to contact him.

I looked up Gerald's name in the Yellow Pages, phoned his business and the call was redirected to his cellphone which he *answered*. He told me he had been in to his business, got all his stock and computers, and had now moved his business into a new location in Papanui Road. I asked Gerald if he knew how I could contact the jeweller with my mother's ring. He didn't, but he thought perhaps *he* remembered valuing the sparkly old thing. He told me he would check his records in case he still had the ring.

He phoned back the next day and told me he had valued the ring on the morning of 22 February and returned it to the jeweller at lunchtime. He also told me the jeweller's name was Ted (Gerald didn't know his surname) and he gave me Ted's home phone number.

Now there was a trail. My mother took the ring to the jeweller named Ted on 17 February. Ted sent one of his shop assistants, with the ring, to Gerald, the valuer across the road, on 18 February. Gerald took photographs of the ring and wrote up the new valuation on the morning of 22 February then he took the ring across the street, back to Ted the jeweller.

Then nothing.

2 April 2011
After phoning several times, I reached Ted's wife. I asked her to ask him to phone me. He didn't so I phoned him. I caught him at home on the third try. I asked him if any of his staff had been killed or hurt in the quake. He said there were a few cuts and grazes, but nothing more serious. He had a broad Devon accent and a defeated air. I distrusted him instantly.

I explained the trail to him and asked him if he had any ideas about what might have happened to the ring.

Was it in his safe? I asked, thinking of a business like the

Mercedes factory where every step would be guided by a protocol that never varied. He told me that he was only the owner and did not actually work there, so he did not know how the ring would have been handled, and he had no idea where the ring would have been at the time of the earthquake. He had not been allowed in to his business since the earthquake, he said. He also said that he might not be continuing in business. I felt as though I was trying to hold on to a small undomesticated animal. It was wriggling and its eyes were darting from side to side, looking for a dark hole it could run away into.

He said he would ask his staff if they remembered the ring and get back to me.

He didn't.

9 April 2011

I phoned Ted again. He repeated that he had not been in to his business and did not know anything about the property which was there at the time of the earthquake. He made no offer to keep in touch, so I said I would phone him weekly to see how things were progressing. I wanted to keep his mind on our problem.

17 April 2011

I rang Ted again. He prevaricated some more. His shop was in Zone 12, he said, as if that was important. The closest he had been to his shop was the fence. Etc. Etc. At one stage he began a vivid description of the minutes straight after the quake.

He and all the staff scrabbling around in the broken glass and bricks, picking up whatever jewellery they could lay their hands on, taking it down to the basement where they had a wall safe. Power off, the basement in total darkness, aftershocks and sirens and people screaming. These were the first things he said which I believed.

They shoved, that was his word, *shoved*, whatever they had in their hands into the safe, but they were only able to lock one of its two locks. After that, he said, the police came and made them leave the building.

I was at a loss to know how to do any more for my mother, who, I now realised, felt guilty that, after three generations, the ring had been lost *on her watch*. Those were her words. My partner and I talked about options. Could you phone the police if you suspected someone of an *intention* to commit a crime? We thought not. What if Ted was not dishonest – just useless? Looking at this now, I see that a couple of weeks went by in this phase. I can think of no reason why so much time passed, when the next step is so obvious.

28 April 2011

I emailed my mother's solicitor for advice. I thought about asking a lawyer near home but decided that a lawyer who was doing business in Christchurch would have more of a feel for what was going on than a lawyer from Paraparaumu. I was imagining Ted in court as I wrote this, so I was careful.

Good morning Kerry

I have made a time to talk with you tomorrow, April 29 at 2.30 about the best way for us to proceed regarding a diamond ring that belongs to my mother and is missing in the earthquake.
The ring was at X Jewellers being valued on Feb 22. There is no dispute about that. The ring is an antique, with sentimental value as well as an insured value of more than $50,000.

My mother has asked me to help her to recover the ring, if at

all possible. At this stage, I am uneasy about the attitude of
Ted X, the business owner, having found him evasive at best
and probably lying once that I am aware of.

I wonder if Ted is making any reasonable effort to locate the
rings and what the standard operating procedure would have
been for handling rings like this – would they always be put
into a safe on return from valuation? And therefore what the
chances are of recovering them from the safe?

And I wonder what is to stop a business owner in this situation
from claiming from his insurance, leaving my mother to claim
from her insurance, and recovering the ring himself?

I imagine the building will soon be demoslished [*sic*]. Once
that happens there is no further chamce [*sic*] to reciver [*sic*] the
rings, so there is possibly some urgency.

I have tried to engage Ted in discussion about the recovery of
the rings but he is not helpful. I have also left a message for the
other owner, Mr B, (17/04/11) asking him to contact me and have
not had a response.

I would like advice about what to do next. I imagine there are
lots of situations a bit like this in Christchurch.

Lynn

1 May 2011

Two days after I spoke with the lawyer, Ted phones. He has
been allowed in to his business for fifteen minutes, during
which time he has retrieved my mother's ring, which he is now
keen to hand over to us. I ask him to keep it until I am next
down in Christchurch, on 23 May. He agrees. I am to phone
him when I arrive in Christchurch.

23 May 2011

I arrive in Christchurch. The shuttle driver tells me there is a vagrant living in the Grand Chancellor Hotel, eating the food and drinking the drinks left behind in 26 storeys of minibars. He follows the sun around the building to keep warm and sleeps in a different room each night, according to the driver.

The hotel building, supported with truckloads of concrete while complex negotiations are going on about who will pay for demolition, is on a clear lean. I see that as we pass nearby. Many of its windows are broken, curtains flap in the wind, and there are stories in the paper of expensive belongings people had left behind in the panic of evacuating the building.

According to the driver, the man was spotted by police as a mobile dark shape on infra-red thermal imaging equipment, the building itself having reached the ambient temperature of Christchurch in May.

After that there are earnest conversations between the passengers about how the man could have got past the cordon and whether he had been homeless before the earthquake or not, the answer to this last question apparently making a huge difference to the whole situation.

24 May 2011

I phone Ted to arrange the handover. He suggests I meet him at 7 p.m. the next evening, in the car park of a disused garden centre in Marshlands Road. I say no to the garden centre car park in the dark. I suggest we meet at a BP petrol station near the garden centre which I assume will be better lit and have more people around. He agrees. Don't forget, he says, there is a charge of $175 for the valuation. Bring a cheque made out to X Jewellers.

25 May 2011

11 a.m.
I ask my mother if she would rather stay home while I go get the ring, but she says no, she wouldn't dream of letting me go by myself.

2 p.m.
We drive out to the BP station, work out the direction Ted will come from and where we can park and watch who is coming and going.

5 p.m.
We put two torches in the car, one with a big heavy handle. We tell two other people where we are going and instruct them to call the police if we are not home by 9 p.m. Down the phone from Raumati, my partner hums the Harry Lime theme.

6.45 p.m.
We arrive at the BP station fifteen minutes early. I park and we begin surveillance. After a while we see one car with a woman driver pull up. I write down its number plate. Then another car, and another, each with a woman driver. I write down all the number plates because when someone finds our car and our battered bodies, the number plates will help them find who did it. Then, about 7.07 p.m., Ted pulls up in an old grey Toyota Corolla. I know it's him because I had asked him what sort of car he drove. We stay in the shadows, watching what is happening. A little pattern emerges. A woman gets out of her car and approaches Ted's car. He gets out and they walk to the rear of his car. In the red light of his tail light, he gets a package out of the boot, unwraps it, shows the woman

something, she signs a piece of paper and goes back to her car. She drives off. After the third woman has driven off, I drive our car up behind Ted's car and leave the lights on. We wait.

He comes over to the driver's window. Lynn? he says. I introduce my mother and myself. Is it OK if I get in the car, he asks. Yes, I say, and he gets into the back seat. I turn the inside car light on. He could easily hit me on the head from behind, and I should have thought of that but now it is too late.

He gets out an envelope. This is the valuation, he says. He hands us photographs of the ring. We hand him the cheque. I get out the big torch and shine it on the photographs. He gets a package out of his pocket, unwraps it and holds the ivory ring box out to my mother. We open the box and compare the ring with the photograph. I ask my mother if she is satisfied that this is her ring. She says yes.

Ted hands her a piece of notepad paper with 'I acknowledge receipt of my ring' written in ballpoint pen. Sign here please, he says. My mother signs.

Ted sighs and folds over somehow. When he starts talking it's all about insurance. You take out insurance and you think you've got yourself covered for everything, he says, and then when something like this happens, you realise that there is so much that you never even thought about. It's all just business, he says. If they have four billion in claims and they can hold on to that money for an extra couple of weeks even, the interest on that is probably the size of my whole claim.

The insurance company is keeping him waiting, he says. He phones them every week and each time he talks to a different person. They won't say whether they will be paying him out. He thinks they are too scared to tell him the decision. He wants them to pay him out for a total loss, he says, but they want to set him up in new premises because that is cheaper for them. If they investigate you, and they find that you needed money *before* the earthquake, they won't pay out, he says. I wonder if the jewellery shop in Cashel Mall was in trouble. I am trying to think of a way to ask that, but by then my mother has had enough of the ancient mariner's story, and she dismisses him rather firmly.

We drive home across the city in the dark. There aren't many of us on the road. To my right, as we drive down Fitzgerald Avenue, I see the Red Zone. Actually I do not see anything. The centre of the city is as dark as the inside of a cow.

Postscript: December 2014

Sometimes I wonder if all this really happened, but, except for the story of the vagrant, it did. I think I made that up. When I wrote the ring story, the week after we retrieved the ring, it had a happy ending. I suppose I assumed there would be many other happy endings in Christchurch. Nearly four years later, there are still families living in sheds, and thousands of others living in their broken houses while they battle their way through the insurance system. Kerry, the kind lawyer who advised us so calmly, has died. All of this makes the return of the ring a nice moment in a big complicated story.

Ross Nepia Himona
Some Thoughts on ANZAC Day

A lot of money has been spent on commemoration, a lot of hype generated and mythology recycled on the occasion of the hundredth anniversary of the ill-fated Gallipoli campaign. And there has been a lot of criticism of this expenditure, hype and mythology. But too many of those who comment today about the relevance of ANZAC and the mythology of ANZAC are walking in their own comfortable shoes instead of in the boots of those World War I warriors. To be understood, history has to be perceived through the eyes of its participants or observers, not just from the distance of a hundred years and through the lens of modern ideology. I try to see World War I through the eyes of my grandfathers.

Grandfather Whana of Ngāti Kere (Pōrangahau) and Ngāti Hikarara (south Wairarapa) didn't enlist for World War I. At that time enlistment was not a popular option for Māori so he was not one of the approximately 2227 Māori who did enlist. By 1914 he was 35 years old, a dairy farmer, and the father of four of his eventual nine children. He had responsibilities at home. We don't know what his views were about the British Empire, but as staunch Mormons who regularly hosted Mormon missionaries in their home in South Wairarapa both he and my grandmother were members of a congregation that directed their attention and allegiance more towards the United States than towards England.

First published on 2 May 2015 on Te Putatara: putatara.net

On the other hand, as a dairy farmer he would have known that he relied on a buoyant New Zealand economy for his livelihood and that depended heavily on continuing sales of primary produce into a stable British market.

Grandfather Fred of East Clive in Hawke's Bay did enlist. He was about the same age as Grandfather Whana and he was a first-generation New Zealander born at Waipūreku a.k.a. East Clive. His father was born in Cornwall and his mother in Devon. They came to New Zealand in 1872 as economic migrants and they were steadfastly British with an abiding loyalty to Mother England. That loyalty was shared by their many children, most of them born in New Zealand. At the start of the war Fred was a single man working as a bushman. He tried to enlist but was rejected because at 37 he was too old. More than two years later when the NZEF needed more recruits he was accepted, joined the Third Battalion of the New Zealand Rifle Brigade on the Western Front, was badly wounded at Passchendaele in October 1917, was invalided to London and after he recovered was sent on light duties to the NZ Rifle Brigade rear echelon at Brocton Camp in Staffordshire. There he remained for the rest of the war, met and married Grandmother Gertrude and eventually came back to New Zealand with his wife and daughter towards the end of 1919.

Grandfather Whana died young, just a few years before World War II – a victim of metabolic diseases brought on by the too rapid adoption of the European lifestyle and the European diet, especially sugar, flour and milk. Ironically, it was the European diet that did for far more of our people than the European wars, and continues to do so to this day. The 1918 European influenza epidemic brought home from the war also did for many more Māori than the war itself. Grandfather

Whana was involved in local efforts to treat the disease and to contain the pandemic.

My father, his son, didn't enlist for World War II. A few of his wider whānau did but not many. Most of his whānau did not get caught up in the fervour of Sir Apirana Ngata's drive to recruit and reinforce the 28th Māori Battalion. Our whānau was still not into other peoples' wars. His best friend, my godfather, did enlist and served on Norfolk Island and then in Italy but in the Army Engineers not in the Māori Battalion. Twenty years on I broke the mould on my Māori side and served in the New Zealand Army for just over twenty years, including active service in Borneo and in South Vietnam.

I march on ANZAC Day. But I cringe at the myth-making and hype surrounding ANZAC these days. I wonder about the tens of thousands who now turn out to dawn services across New Zealand and Australia. Are they there to mourn or are they there to bask in the hype and to celebrate the mythology fed to them by politicians and media? How many of them really know or fully understand why they are there? I march for simple and clear reasons.

I don't march in remembrance of the dead of the New Zealand Wars, for reasons I will explain later. However, I do mourn the loss of land, whether through war and confiscation or through questionable sale. But I'm not sure how we might memorialise that, or even if we should.

Grandfather Fred was like a great many men who went to war for New Zealand and Australia and who were either born in Britain or were the children of British parents. He would have felt it his bounden duty to rise to the defence of the British Empire. His generation were becoming New Zealanders but still staunchly British. The evolutionary process of becoming New Zealanders took a long time. We didn't gain New Zealand citizenship until 1948, thirty years after World War I and three years after World War II. Up until then we were British subjects, and from 1948 until 1983 we were British subjects and New Zealand citizens. I remember as a child in the 1950s that most of my Pākehā schoolmates were still proud to be British subjects.

It is easy to look backwards a hundred years after Gallipoli and decry the folly of going to the other side of the world to fight a war that in no way threatened New Zealand's shores, in campaigns – often badly conceived campaigns – that senselessly slaughtered millions of young men. But I see World War I through the perspective of Grandfather Fred and through the perspective of his times. He went out of duty and loyalty to England and to his British Empire. It was his war, not someone else's war. I honour him for that.

He may also have gone for the adventure and to visit the land of his forefathers. Having signed up for a bit of travel and adventure myself 45 years later I can understand that too.

So in this second decade of the twenty-first century, what do I think of ANZAC?

I grew up with ANZAC. As a school cadet in the 1950s and early 1960s I was proud to be a uniformed member of catafalque parties at country memorials on ANZAC Day. When I was a teenager in uniform World War II was just ten years gone, the Korean War had just ended and the Malayan Emergency was still going. Grandfather Fred, veteran of World War I, died about that time, well into his eighties. ANZAC Day was a funeral, not a celebration of anything except perhaps the lives of those who died. It was a mourning of the dead, including the very recent dead, by families, comrades and communities.

None of those war memorials in cities, towns and villages were erected to glorify war or to glorify sacrifice or to promote militarism or to celebrate the defence of freedom and liberty. They were erected as substitute tombstones for the thousands of soldiers who lie buried in foreign lands, some in unmarked graves. They became the focus of mourning for a country lacking graves and headstones and the ability to travel to where the dead lay. ANZAC Day was not about celebrating a failed campaign in the Dardanelles, or the mythical founding of a nation, or a celebration of democratic values or the gallantry of the ANZAC soldier. All of that is legend or mythology. ANZAC Day was a service for the dead. Its ritual was and is still the solemn ritual of a military funeral.

It was also and remains an annual reunion for those whose incredibly strong bonds of trust, brotherhood and comradeship were forged in war. Only the veteran knows the power and the strength of that bond. In that sense everyone else is an onlooker or a bystander.

That remains for me the meaning of ANZAC Day. I remember and honour the dead and the physically and psychologically wounded of all wars. I honour too all who fought in those wars, especially those whānau and friends who have since faded away. Regardless of the strategic, political and economic necessity or futility of those wars I honour the casualties of the wars, both the dead and the living. I remember and honour Grandfather Fred.

I honour also Grandfather Whana's and my father's decisions not to fight other peoples' wars. Their loyalties rightly lay elsewhere.

For me the debate about the necessity or futility of war – past, present and future – is for every other week of the year. Raising that debate in ANZAC week, even in response to the

maddening hype and mythology, is just as inappropriate as
the hype and mythology. Like the tangihanga itself, ANZAC
week is a time for restraint and respect.

However, in that larger debate I do decry the political and
commercial appropriation of ANZAC for base motives that
dishonour the dead. We should read the academic military
historians to learn the unadorned facts about ANZAC.
But their work does not seep into popular consciousness.
Not many are interested. What does pass as fact is the work
of popular historians who perpetuate and reinforce the prop-
aganda and mythology of ANZAC and who along with
politicians and the media distort reality and so shape false
perceptions for the next generations.

So what about the call to mourn, say, the dead of the New
Zealand Wars on ANZAC Day, as well as the dead of the more
recent wars?

Well, down our way Grandfather Whana's father and grandfather didn't go to war to try to keep their lands. They didn't
have a strong enough military base. They lost their lands
mostly – but not always – by reluctant sale. The New Zealand
Wars, like the later world wars, were other peoples' wars.
Indeed, some of the tribes who did fight actually fought on the
side of the settler government. And some of those were also
the tribes who made the greatest contributions to the Māori
Battalion of World War II. No doubt they had their reasons but
it might not be profitable to mine that seam too deep.

Some forty years before the New Zealand Wars our rohe
was infested by marauding hapū during the Musket Wars
attempting to dispossess the many hapū of our lands. They
initially succeeded but were eventually repulsed as we acquired
muskets and as the missionaries intervened. No doubt some
of my tīpuna would not have been at all inclined to mourn

the dead of those invading hapū in the New Zealand Wars. We don't all share a common history.

So I'm a bit ambivalent about commemorating other tribes' wars, whatever side they fought on. But if those tribes want to set aside their own day of mourning that's OK by me. Mourning the loss of land might be something we could have in common. It would be a bit like mourning the loss of lives in war, I suppose. It sounds like a good idea but it's a bit more complex than it sounds.

Should we really set aside a day to mourn what divided my two grandfathers, or seek instead to celebrate what joins us? Much modern-day ANZAC belief lies in the myth that New Zealand came of age or achieved nationhood on the World War I battlefields, especially Gallipoli. Of course it's pure rubbish. Grandfather Whana's people were here in this land for some 700 years before Gallipoli. Grandfather Fred's people were here for about 150 years before Gallipoli. We try to celebrate the joining of these two strands of migration on Waitangi Day – not very successfully, because we are still divided over what Waitangi means to the nation as a whole. Grandfather Whana seems to be pulling in one direction and Grandfather Fred in another.

They never met, but as men of the land I'm sure they would have found much in common. A shared love of the land perhaps; the farmer and the bushman. Neither of them was much interested in politics. Grandfather Fred, like most of his generation, didn't much like Māori. He did change his attitude a bit after he acquired a Māori son-in-law and Māori mokopuna. Incidentally, he didn't much like Catholics either and didn't ever approve of his Pākehā Catholic son-in-law. Those were his times. Grandfather Whana didn't go to war but I'm sure he would have understood and honoured

Grandfather Fred's decision. He did after all name one of his daughters Lemnos Mudros, after the island and its harbour from where the Gallipoli campaign was launched. I've no idea why. It's a mystery.

I've no idea either how we might celebrate the real birth of this nation formed primarily from twin strands of migration through a clash of cultures, a short period of armed conflict in some parts, a long period of inter-cultural political and economic turmoil in most parts, and an even longer aftermath through which we are still finding our way. Perhaps if we're patient the answer will in time reveal itself. Perhaps it will be in finally cutting the ties to monarchy and all it represents and in the birth of a new republic. Our day of celebration of nationhood might lie not in the past but in the future.

In the meantime, let ANZAC Day remain simply a mourning for our dead in the conflicts where a lot of us fought on the same side, for whatever reason.

Lest we forget.

Kate Camp
From the Uttermost Ends of the Earth

There's a cold in Europe that's different from the cold in New Zealand. It isn't coming up from the ground, or carried in the wind. It's like it's already inside you, and no matter how many clothes you have on, after half an hour all you can think about is getting indoors. I am astonished that anyone survived the wars of Europe. Even without the gas, gunfire, shelling, rats and disease, just surviving the weather is unimaginable.

Ypres is a beautiful town. Or maybe I should say, Ypres was a beautiful town, and the new Ypres, rebuilt brick by brick after World War I, is beautiful too. It's an almost exact replica but with more room for parking.

I checked in to my hotel which had the rare luxury of a kettle in the room, reflecting how many English tourists pass through. As I ate my omelette in a café off the town square, I watched an elderly couple. He ordered steak and frites, and she had the mussels: a huge, two-tiered steamer affair, full of the tiny Belgian mussels that are so time-consuming to eat compared to our New Zealand ones, but so tender and delicious. They each had a glass of wine. How very European, I caught myself thinking, and maybe it was, because she was wearing shoes with heels and was dressed in black. He was either wearing a beret, or my imagination has inserted one in the intervening years.

First published on 16 August 2014 in the New Zealand Book Council's journal *Booknotes Unbound*: booknotes-unbound.org.nz

Having signed up for a minivan tour of the battlefields, I found myself with seven Dutch tourists and our Belgian guide. Humiliatingly, the Dutch majority opted to have the tour in English, for my benefit.

There are so many things that will break your heart when you think about the fighting in Belgium. The bunkers by the canals where doctors operated their butcher's shops. The gas attacks that left the ground littered with rabbits, mice and moles, driven from their holes by the low-rolling cloud. The gravestones laid out in groups – when a number of men were killed at once, so that the parts of their bodies were all mixed up, the collective remains would be buried together and the gravestones set in a row, touching each other, like a row of teeth.

But the thing I find most depressing is how flat everything is, how unimpressive and undistinguished it is as a landscape. Here is a ridge that changed hands a dozen times: it's a hump in the ground not much higher than a railway crossing. Here is the famous wood that cost hundreds of lives – it's just a bunch of trees, like you'd get on some scrap of land down the back of a farm.

I'd read about the battles for the high ground, for Hill 60, for vantage points unassailable to the enemy. But to my New Zealand eyes, my Wellington eyes, the whole place looks so flat and anonymous. It's like there's no real geography, just names and lines on land as level as a map.

Our guide does a great job. He has copies of letters and diaries with him, which he reads from, and aerial photos of the area after the war. It looks like something under a microscope, like the surface of an atom. One of the letters talks about the destruction being so absolute, that the locations of villages could only be identified by brick-coloured stains on the ground. There is something very haunting about the way that trees and medieval churches and goats and men and cellars and blades of grass were all pulverised and mixed up together, 'as in a mortar and pestle'.

(This is a quote from Ernst Junger's memoir *Storm of Steel*, which I buy in Ypres town later that day, and read that night. The trip and the book will always be tied together in my mind.)

We visit some of the New Zealand memorials, which are dotted around, apart from the other monuments. They always say: FROM THE UTTERMOST ENDS OF THE EARTH. It is very affecting, but also, infuriating. It is so insane to die in war, but to travel so far around the globe for that purpose? And there's something about that phrase, 'the uttermost ends of the earth' that annoys me too, because it is this battlefield, this war that was the uttermost: this was the end of the earth.

New Zealand war memorials are always separate from the others, because New Zealand decided that the graves should be as close as possible to where the men had fallen. The effect of this is that they can be hard to find, and when you do find them, they might be just there at the junction of two country roads, next to a give way sign, or with a sheet metal factory nearby.

As you drive around, you sometimes see old shell casings left by road signs. They still dig them up and they are left out for the authorities to collect. Every now and again they find a big one, or one goes off and kills someone, our guide says.

Tyne Cot is the big Commonwealth cemetery. By the time we arrive, it's so cold we all have drips on our noses and watering eyes. It's a kind of ersatz emotion, because it's hard to feel much in the cemetery, having already been to so many more intimate sites of death and suffering.

The sun's come out by the time we get to the German cemetery, Langemark. Unlike the Commonwealth war graves,

German war cemeteries are rarely visited. For obvious reasons, the Germans don't go in much for war memorials, war tourism, looking up the old relatives. But of course these dead Germans are the 'good' ones. The remains of 44,000 World War I German soldiers are interred here in a mass grave.

I get a shock when I see paper poppies on one of the German graves, with a wreath. I should know this from reading *All Quiet on the Western Front*, how you forget that it's the same war, on the same ground, in many ways the exact same experience. And, of course, the same flowers.

In fact, I always thought that *All Quiet on the Western Front* was an English book about English soldiers. I was a quarter of the way through the novel, when Paul is heading home on the eastward-bound train, before it dawned on me he was German.

Before we leave Langemark, I use the public toilet, although it is bitterly cold. I tell our guide that my mother taught me never to pass up the chance to use a toilet. He says his mother taught him the exact same thing.

Back in Ypres the streets are decorated for Christmas, with stars of white fairy lights strung across the narrow pedestrian street that leads down to the Menin Gate. There has been a service there every night since the end of the war. My guide said that when the Nazis occupied Ypres, the service was stopped, but it was re-started by Poles five days later as soon as the town was retaken.

At least that's how I remember the story. It might have been five months. And maybe they weren't Poles, maybe I just have Poles in my head because a few weeks earlier I'd made a trip to Warsaw, and stayed in another beautiful, ancient city that had been rebuilt from scratch after being bombed to dust.

Sometimes it feels like Europe is one big cemetery.

*

Note: *Storm of Steel* is the classic war memoir by German novelist and officer, Ernst Junger. I had never heard of it until I saw it in a bookshop in Ypres, but it has become one of those books that I now force on people. Everyone I know who has read it has been staggered by it.

In the new translation by Michael Hofmann, it has what the blurb of this edition quite rightly refers to as an 'ashen lyricism', as seen in its opening passage:

> The train stopped at Bazancourt, a small town in Champagne, and we got out. Full of awe and incredulity, we listened to the slow, grinding pulse of the front, a rhythm we were to become mightily familiar with over the years. The white ball of a shrapnel shell melted far off, suffusing the grey December sky. The breath of battle blew across to us, and we shuddered. Did we sense that almost all of us – some sooner, some later – were to be consumed by it, on days when the dark grumbling yonder would crash over our heads like an incessant thunder?

Charles Anderson
Into the Black: The *Easy Rider* Story

He awakes alone in the black at 12.03 a.m. He does not look at the clock but he knows the time. He cannot see their faces but he knows who they are. The silhouettes surround him in silence. He is not afraid. He closes his eyes and remembers their story. It is his too.

He remembers the taste of salt, the smell of gasoline, the constant slap of water against his skin. He remembers what absolute loneliness feels like.

He will say he was ready to die. He will say his entire life led up to the moment when he decided not to.

There were nine, including him. They had set out together on a boat called the *Easy Rider*. The only difference in their story is that he is alive and they are not.

The harbour

The strait spat grey and cold as Rewai 'Spud' Karetai made his way across Fisherman's Wharf. There were supplies to be organised and bait to be loaded but to some who saw him he seemed preoccupied. His fishing boat, the *Easy Rider*, was

This story is based on extensive interviews and hundreds of pages of documents including court files, Transport Accident Investigation Commission reports and coroner's inquiries. Fairfax Media gained access to never before seen material including audio recordings made by the commission in the disaster's aftermath and logbooks from the search. Scenes and dialogue not observed by the reporter were taken from information and direct recollections from these sources. First published in 2014 as an interactive on the Stuff website: stuff.co.nz/interactives/2014/into-the-black tied up along with dozens of others that bobbed on Bluff Harbour's ebbing tide.

It is one of the few safe inlets in the Foveaux Strait but entering it is still a challenge. Its waters move swiftly and its winds blow strong. There are rocks that lurk beneath the surface. When boats finally reach the passage between the mainland and Stewart Island they are often faced with bruised clouds and white-capped waves. This is Southland – the bottom of New Zealand where State Highway 1 peters out. But according to signage on the roadside, Bluff and its population 1824 people really mark the 'beginning of the journey'.

Karetai had bought the *Easy Rider* only six months earlier and he was proud of it. Most of his life had been on fishing vessels. The sea was his playground, friends said. It was in his bones. He had spent thirty years as a deckhand, helping run ships around the southern edge of the country but the *Easy Rider* was different. He and his wife Gloria wanted to be their own bosses and to run their own commercial fishing operation. The *Easy Rider* would be the first boat Karetai would ever captain.

On 14 March 2012 Karetai spent the morning loading up stores – 2.1 tonnes of ice and 360 kilograms of bait.

Maritime New Zealand safety inspector Gary Levy was on his way to audit a nearby vessel at Fisherman's Wharf when, just after lunch, he stopped by to inspect the *Easy Rider*.

Levy was there to make sure Karetai's boat met 'safe ship compliance'. The *Easy Rider* had been privately owned for many years and for Karetai to use it commercially several standards had to be met.

It needed a lot of work. But the most essential element was someone in control who held a skipper's certificate. Without it the 42-year-old, 11-metre boat would not be permitted to carry any passengers.

While it was Gloria's name on the ownership forms, Karetai had run the *Easy Rider* largely by himself. Several deckhands helped out occasionally but in six months Karetai had already gone through seven different men. He had a reputation for being hard to work for and not someone you could easily tell what to do.

He also had not completed his own skipper's certificate which required him to pass courses in, among other things, boat stability. So since purchasing the boat he had used his only qualification – a deckhand certificate.

Levy asked to see a full copy of the licences. Karetai started to look around the boat. Then he rang his wife and put her on speaker phone. Was his skipper's ticket in a cupboard, he asked. It wasn't, Gloria said.

Then Karetai told Levy he would need to go home to look for it.

Levy tried to complete the inspection but he thought the whole thing was 'turning into a farce'. The weather was closing in, the forecast was not looking good and from what Karetai was telling him Levy thought there was no chance of the *Easy Rider* leaving the harbour.

MetService warned of 35 knot winds. The seas would become rough for a time with a swell rising to 4 metres.

If Levy had known Karetai was thinking about leaving, he later told a court, he would have detained the vessel.

As Levy left, a truck driven by two of Karetai's relatives, Paul Karetai and Peter Bloxham, pulled into the port. It was carrying stores and materials including plywood and corrugated iron sheets.

Wood was craned up and lowered onto the *Easy Rider*. The vessel listed heavily to one side. The crane then repositioned the load until the boat appeared to be stable.

At 5 p.m., David Hawkless, a fisherman with fifty years' experience in the Foveaux, passed the *Easy Rider* on his way back into the harbour. Hawkless thought he wouldn't want to take a boat out with that much gear on it. He would tell his wife that night that the *Easy Rider* seemed low in the water and that it was 'dangerously overloaded'.

He did not know, however, that there would be other people, more weight, coming aboard.

Later that day, about 7.30 p.m., deckhands Shane Topi and Dallas Reedy arrived. Karetai called them 'eight' and 'nine' – the latest men to work for him. They loaded fuel tanks and filled the fresh water barrel.

Reedy was number nine – a solid man with a greying goatee. Originally from the North Island's east coast, he once played rugby league for Southland. Reedy bounced around fishing jobs, from Tasmania to Antarctica, before joining Karetai on the *Easy Rider*. He had known Karetai for years and he knew how to handle him. If he was 'in a mood' Reedy would just move to the other end of the boat to let him calm down. It was hard work but Reedy trusted Spud.

The planned trip was to take some of Karetai's relatives out to the Tītī or Muttonbird Islands – an archipelago at the bottom of Stewart Island. They were to go hunting for muttonbirds, also known as young sooty shearwaters, which nested there. It was a tradition passed down to local Māori for generations. Karetai would then continue on to fish before returning to pick up the passengers. They would all return to Bluff together.

Paul Karetai and Peter Bloxham had arranged that week for Rewai to take them down to the islands. But soon after, other family members arrived at the harbour. Every one of them aside from Reedy were related.

Gloria thought her husband might have felt some pressure to help them out with the expensive eight-hour boat trip. Whatever the reason, Boe Gilles, John Karetai and Dave Fowler all came aboard. The deck was so tightly packed that Reedy and Topi could only access the sides of the load by standing on the boat's outer railings.

Then, Paul Fowler-Karetai arrived with his seven-year-old son Odin.

Fowler had not planned on making the trip but thought that it would be just a few days. He jumped aboard. Odin started to cry and pleaded with his father. He wanted to go too.

'Come on Dad,' he said.

'Nah, sorry son.'

The boat was ready to go. Reedy and Topi had lashed down the loads and were making moves to cast off. At the last moment, Fowler-Karetai changed his mind.

'Come on then mate, hop aboard.'

Odin grinned. Reedy thought the boy looked cold so he put a small black lifejacket on him.

'This will make you look cool,' he told him.

At about 8 p.m. Karetai fired up the boat's four-cylinder diesel engine. As the vessel manoeuvred away from shore someone on the opposite quay noted that there was already water sloshing on to the deck.

Karetai called Bluff Fisherman's Radio and told them he was heading to the Muttonbird Islands but did not say in which direction. For some reason he also said there were only seven people aboard.

'Good as gold,' the message came back from the radio's long-time operator Meri Leask.

Then Karetai steered the vessel through the channel before turning west and out into the strait.

Shipwrecks and the strait

The anchor sits just off State Highway 1 before the road winds its final journey towards Bluff. It is thick and rusted and embedded in red brick. It is introduced with words from Psalm 130 – etched into the face of a granite slab.

'Out in the depths I cry to you O Lord.'

Around it are brass plaques with names and dates and flowers. It is a memorial to those who have been lost at sea. There is Arthur Fisher, the beloved husband, father and skipper of the *Golden Harvest* who was lost in 1968. There is Roger Burgess, lost off the *Cygnet* in 1985, Basil Mortimer lost at sea off the *Skagen*. But long before the memorial was created or those men lost, ships have foundered in the Foveaux Strait.

It takes only twelve minutes for a storm to manifest itself in the waves. The strait sits at the pressure point between the Mariana Trench, where seas belch up from 10,000 metres deep, and the 6000-metre-deep waters summoned from around Cape Horn in the other direction. They collide in the 40-metre shallows of the Foveaux.

The strait turns, say Bluff fishermen, into a washing machine. The prevailing weather is westerly but the tide runs east to west. When they hit each other, even in no wind, the water will just 'stand up', says local coastguard president Andy Johnson.

'These are waves with nothing on the back of them. They are just walls of water.'

They turned over cargo carriers and passenger vessels that arrived in Bluff during the nineteenth century when it was just an outpost built on trade. The local museum houses an unofficial honour roll of sunken ships. In glass cases are salvaged materials – broken pieces of wooden hull and never drunk bottles of stout beer.

At least 125 boats have gone down since 1831. At least 74 people have perished but the real number is not clear. It is still ticking over. Six years earlier, in 2006, another boat, the *Kotuku*, was on its way back from the Tītī Islands after mutton-birding. The tradition stretched back to before the 1840 Treaty of Waitangi where the right to continue the trip was enshrined. Families of Rakiura Māori, who had direct blood lines to the early chiefs of Stewart Island, held that right in perpetuity.

They knew the strait as Te Ara a Kiwa or the pathway of Kiwa – an ancestor who, according to legend, asked a whale to create a passage of water by eating through the land. Crumbs that fell from the whale's mouth became the islands in the strait – including the Tītīs.

There was something about them that drew those ancestors back. It was a link to their past when muttonbirding was vital for trade. In the early days Māori would travel by paddle-driven waka. Then came motorised boats. More recently helicopters have been enlisted to help lift stores off the boats and onto the islands. But this means most materials had to be secured on the deck rather than in a hold.

For three months every year the islands could be inhabited. Families each had their own 'manu' or area which they hunted and makeshift houses grew there over the years. Different family members would bring down wood and supplies to build on to them.

Some had television and internet but the focus was fishing out the birds, which burrowed into the peaty surface of the islands, with sticks with hooks on the end. The birds' greasy meat was considered a delicacy and a rarity.

Through generations, it remained one of the most isolated places in the country.

The islands are special, Andy Johnson says. They have a feel about them and a certain sweet smell. Local Māori are vigorously protective of what is still, for many, a rite of passage.

On that day in 2006, before the *Kotuku* made it back to Bluff, the boat was swamped by a wave. An investigation found it was unstable and overloaded. Six people drowned. Three others managed to swim to a nearby island.

Those waves have even turned over normally stable twin-hull catamarans which is where, three months before setting out on the *Easy Rider*, Rewai Karetai came to intimately know the dangers of the strait.

It was January and he was sleeping in a tent on Ruapuke Island which sits in the middle of the Foveaux. His wife woke him at 10.40 p.m. Gloria was sure she could hear someone in the water. It was loud and the wind was flapping at the tent. She must be mistaken, he told her. Gloria was adamant. So Karetai got up and looked out to the sea. He could see something bobbing on the waves. At first, he thought it could be a cardboard box. As his eyes adjusted he could see it was something else – a lifejacket. Then he heard voices.

They belonged to two women who were holding up another man – Barry Bethune. Karetai rowed out in a small dinghy. He knew they would all try to clamber aboard which would have spilled every one of them into the water.

'You climb into this dinghy,' he said. 'I'm going to hit you with this oar.'

Bethune, the boat's owner, had been looking the other way when the wave hit. He felt the boat getting picked up and tipped over. The other passenger said all she saw was a 'wall of water' – two or three times bigger than any other they had seen that day. There was no time to react. It was known as a 'rogue wave'.

By the time Karetai began rowing the trio to shore two others, including Bethune's son, were dead. Karetai was sure

his father was going to die too. 'Don't give in now,' Karetai
told him. 'I'll club you with this oar.'

Simple things could have saved them all, Karetai told a
reporter after the ordeal. If only they had checked in with
Meri Leask to let her know when they were going out and
when they expected to be back. If only they had a cellphone
and plastic bag to keep it from getting wet. A $2 bag would
have saved them, he said.

'You need to respect Foveaux Strait. If you don't respect it, it
will kill you.'

On the boat

It was midnight and the Radio New Zealand broadcaster
began announcing the day's headlines. The *Easy Rider* was
punching into the tide as it neared the northwestern point of
Stewart Island. It bounced over waves and slid over their tips
before slamming down onto the ocean below.

Dallas Reedy looked over to the two others on deck and
laughed to himself. Under a quarter moon Boe Gilles and
Pete Bloxham were faring badly. They opened a box of beers
and starting sipping on them, hoping to calm their stomachs.
Dallas had a few too and started to relax into the evening.
There was little room on deck so he settled against two blue
plastic water barrels. It was going to be a long trip, he thought.

Rewai was at the wheel alongside Dave Fowler. Next to
Karetai was an emergency indicating radio beacon. Once
activated it transmitted a global positioning message to 100
metres accuracy. If it was above water, satellites could pick up
its message and relay it to the Rescue Coordination Centre
that managed all ocean emergencies around the country.
But to work it had to be switched on manually.

The other deckhand, Shane Topi, had already gone down

into the cabin below to sleep. Two months earlier, the first time Reedy met Topi, he asked him if he liked the water.

'I hate it,' Topi told him. 'If I fell over I'd probably freak out and freeze.'

Reedy had seen Karetai on television after the tragedy with Barry Bethune became national news. Reedy called him up and asked for a job. He started the next day. Paul Fowler-Karetai and his son were also inside. Reedy thought young Odin looked like he was having the time of his life.

The news bulletin was wrapping up.

'That is your headlines to three minutes past midnight,' the announcer said.

Then Reedy heard it. It sounded like a jet engine. It was a roar from the starboard side. He could not see it coming but within seconds he felt it. The entire deck was swamped. He heard Odin scream and then nothing. The water was up to his waist. Then the *Easy Rider* heeled back and over. In an instant it was upside down and pots and ropes were all around him. Reedy went under. He flailed and tried to grab a rope. All he was wearing was a yellow and blue Stormline jacket, track pants and boots. As soon as he hit the water his boots and pants were sucked off.

The sea temperature was 13 degrees. An adult male wearing a lifejacket could be expected to survive for up to five hours before succumbing to muscle fatigue, cramps and hypothermia. But without a lifejacket, in the cold, Reedy thought he was going to drown.

He fumbled around him for anything to help him stay afloat. He managed to get ahold of a rope that was attached to the boat. The waves pulled him around, slamming him into the side of the hull. It was slippery and barnacled like a whale but he knew he had to stay out of the water for as long as possible.

He clambered aboard and wedged himself between the propeller and the rudder as waves continued to crash over him. It felt like death was coming for him.

There was no moon. No stars. Only the boat's light still attached to a battery. After fifteen minutes it went black. Then came the cold. He looked around and could see no one. He banged on the hull with his fists hoping to get a reply from those who were in the cabins. He yelled. There was nothing – only the sound of the ocean.

The *Easy Rider*'s dinghy was still tied up – only metres away. But if he didn't reach it or if he could not unleash it, Reedy thought he would likely drown. So he sat on the hull, occasionally getting up to squat to get his blood moving.

Two hours passed. He knew he was alone. Then came another sound. It was a *wooosh*. It was like a last, dying breath, Reedy thought. It was the air escaping from the boat. Then the *Easy Rider* tipped vertical and began to sink. He positioned himself on the back of the boat. Then, when the water was up to his knees, he stepped off into the black, the dinghy still tied to the *Easy Rider*, the light from the emergency locator beacon still attached in the ship's wheelhouse, both slowly sinking and fading beneath him.

The search

Chris Green scanned the scene at Big South Cape. It was a perfect day in the Tītī Islands. The sea was a green calm and the sun was shining. The helicopter pilot was there to help lift muttonbirders' loads from their boats and onto the islands. It was a job he had done for many years for various families. That morning, however, something did not seem right. One of his clients was not there. He radioed the *Easy Rider* to find its location but there was no answer.

Then he radioed his office in Te Anau to see if they had received a message from Karetai's wife. Green had spoken to Rewai a few days earlier and suggested he might want to postpone the trip because the weather was not looking good. Karetai told him he was going fishing after stopping at the islands and would not put it off.

But when Green arrived he could not see the *Easy Rider*. He thought maybe Karetai had changed his mind. Green's office rang Gloria who told them that the boat left as expected the previous evening.

At 3.25 p.m. he radioed Meri Leask, who had voluntarily manned the fisherman's radio for more than thirty years. She was already at the Bluff police station on another of her volunteer jobs. She informed the officers there and, in a notepad, logged an overdue vessel.

Green refuelled and then started a coastline search. Perhaps they had stopped in a cove to get some sleep. Perhaps the *Easy Rider* had broken down somewhere along the way. He spoke to the other skippers who had made the trip, one who told him that the boat had been having engine problems. But none of them had seen the *Easy Rider*.

'There was no reason to think anything had gone wrong,' Green said.

But as he went further up the side of Stewart Island he was running out of places where Karetai might have stopped. Then, as he came round the last corner of the island's north-western tip, he noticed a discolouration in the water. Green hovered closer to the surface. He could smell it – diesel. It was bubbling up from below. Close by were plastic bags, plastic petrol cans and, finally, a cabin door.

It was 5 p.m. What none of them knew was that the boat the door belonged to had gone down almost eighteen hours earlier.

Leask transferred to Invercargill Police Station, a fifteen-minute drive away, where a search management team was being organised. An emergency message went out to vessels in the area. Fishing boats and ferries all lent their services. None of them expected to be paid for their work – they did it on the understanding that one day it might be them being looked for.

Rhys Ferguson was just finishing work at the port when he heard his pager go off.

'Missing vessel, Foveaux Strait area,' it read.

The 29-year-old had belonged to the Bluff Coastguard for seven years after a friend encouraged him to volunteer. Usually when a message like that came through it was serious. He knew the strait was not forgiving. The 7-metre coastguard boat was only a short drive away – tied up close to where the *Easy Rider* had set out from. Ferguson was the first there. He opened his locker, grabbed his thermal suit and lifejacket and made preparations to leave. Soon three other volunteers were on board including veteran coastguard skipper Bill Ryan. When the message went out, coastguard president Andy Johnson had called him to tell him extra details.

'If it's in Big South Cape we aren't going,' Ryan told him. 'Our boat would get down there but it won't get back.' The weather was picking back up. If the wind had been only 5 knots stronger they would not have gone at all. The first priority was the safety of their volunteers.

They did not know about the diesel slick that had been discovered to the far west. So when they got out of the harbour they headed straight for Stewart Island.

In the water
He is alone in the black. There is nothing about him. He can barely see a metre. He believes he is about to die.

Almost immediately it pops to the surface – a 20-litre red plastic petrol canister. Nothing else. If it was a little further away he would not have seen it. He slides his fingers through the grip and holds on tight.

Dallas Reedy has been in enough cells by himself to know exactly what an hour is. He can feel it. He believes two have gone by since the wave hit. The boat has just disappeared below him. It is 2 a.m.

The morning. If he can make it to morning then that is his best chance. Did Spud get a mayday out? Did anyone get out? He knows nothing but he knows the water. He has spent most of his life in it. He learned to dive near here – getting in the ocean with great white sharks that returned to these waters around Stewart Island every year. He knows they are out there. He looks down to his hands. His knuckles are bleeding. For a moment he panics. He flails and tries to pull his legs into his chest. He wills himself to be calm. He wills himself to breathe.

He has been cold before. He was in the army in Waiōuru – a tank commander in the bitter winters forced to stay over-night inside the freezing steel. More than once he fell victim to hypothermia. You do that a few times over the years and you learn about your body.

In the dark he has no reference point. He does not know where he is. He puts the boys that were aboard the boat out of his mind. He has to. He can't think about them. He has to survive.

He thinks back to his two sons at home snuggling into their beds, no idea that their father is out in the ocean fighting for his life. He wants them to know that he is. The thought keeps him alive.

Hold on, he tells himself, don't let go. *Hold on. Don't let go.*

He sees things in the water. Millions of them – they sparkle and twinkle in the night. The bioluminescent marine life is the only light he has seen in hours. When he splashes his hand the light disappears. Even out here with all this death, he thinks, there is life.

He is not hungry. Only thirsty. The water slaps against him and tries to force itself into his mouth. He spits and sputters and tries to force it out. His stomach is cramping. He keeps passing stool. Each one more painful than the last. It feels like his body is shutting down.

He thinks about his life. His early days putting in fence posts on the east coast of the North Island. His time in the army and how it gave structure to a kid who had known little. He remembers when he left and the mistakes he made. He remembers the assault on the taxi driver that put him in prison. He remembers meeting Spud there. He remembers playing rugby league on the concrete where inmates would try and smash his teeth out in every tackle. He remembers inmates hanging themselves in the cells next door.

He remembers wanting to turn his life around and do the best for his kids and his wife. He remembers moving to Southland. All of it, he thinks, has led to this moment.

He slips beneath the surface of the ocean. Below him he sees rainbows of colours that remind him of when he fished near Antarctica and saw the Aurora Australis painted across the sky. It is beautiful, he thinks. The hours tick by.

The sun finally hauls itself over the horizon. Dallas believes it is 6 a.m. It looks like the world being born, he thinks. It hits his skin. Finally, he feels warmth. He has lasted the night. Now, he tells himself, someone will find me.

His tongue is swollen. He cannot swallow. The salt water he has been spitting out is seeping into his body.

The waves slap on his jacket. *Slap, slap, slap.* It is constant. *Slap, slap, slap.* JUST F****** STOP! He shouts into the open air.

The ocean does not listen. He tries to concentrate. He looks about him. All this time, land has only been about 3 kilometres away. He cannot see anything else, only land. He has to swim. He moves to take off his jacket. He slides his arms out and lays it flat on the surface. He hopes it will be a signal to helicopters or planes that will come looking for him. Just before he lets go of it he thinks back to a television show he watched once about survival. It was hosted by former special forces soldier Bear Grylls who told his audience to use everything about them to survive. Just before he lets go of the jacket he pulls out the drawstring from its hood. The jacket floats for a second. Then it sinks into the sea.

Dallas ties the string around his wrist and around the petrol canister's grip. *Hold on. Don't let go.*

He awakes beneath the sea. His vision is blurry through the water. The string saves him. He bursts to the surface and into tears. I am dying now he thinks. He passes another stool. It is black.

He has to move. He starts swimming, pushing out the canister with each stroke. It tires him. He stops and ties the string to the elastic of his underwear. He starts for land again. Forty minutes pass. He looks up and sees he is no closer. The current is holding him still. He tries again but each time his energy is drained and he starts to shiver. He looks back to the sun. It is dipping. He has about four hours. He knows he can't fight the current. He knows he can't make it another night.

He begins to sing. Anything at first – songs from the '60s and '70s – the Eagles, Dire Straits. He recites hakas – war challenges he learned as a boy at boarding school. He tells himself jokes. He makes himself laugh. He talks to the petrol canister.

He has named it Wilson, after a Tom Hanks movie he once watched. He feels like he might be losing his mind.

He thinks Wilson is too heavy. There is liquid still inside. Maybe if he can pour some out it will float better. He unscrews the lid like a man defusing a bomb. He begins to tip it out but does not realise how much is still inside. The gasoline pours all over his face and into his eyes. He is blind. He grips the lid in his fist. If he loses it, he will die. Carefully, he screws it back on and begins to say goodbye to everyone he has ever known. Strangers, friends and family – he wishes them all a long life. He begins to say hello to everyone he knows who has already passed over. He says he will see them soon. He is calm.

He tries to untie the string and wrap it around his neck. He wants to keep his head above the water. If he is going to die he wants his mother to be able to have an open-casket funeral. If he sinks beneath the water he knows the sea lice will eat his eyes first. But his hands are too cold. He cannot undo the knot. He tugs at it and rips his underwear off. Naked in the ocean, he fears the sea lice might want to eat something else too.

Then he sees a plane flying high above him. He tries to wave, he tries to scream. It passes by.

When the sun had come up he felt so much hope. It gave him warmth. Now, he can feel it turning on him as it skulks back over the horizon. I can't fight anymore, he thinks. He says goodbye and closes his eyes. He has done enough. He has done enough.

Then he hears it. *Neeeeeeeeeeeeeeeeeeee*. He looks up and locks eyes with a spectacled young man on the back of the boat who speaks words he will never forget: 'SURVIVOR IN THE WATER.'

The rescue

Rhys Ferguson gripped the steel bar outside the coastguard boat wheelhouse. The swell had picked up in the strait. The vessel launched off waves and crashed into the sea. It rocked and rolled. Fishermen who occasionally came aboard during searches would say they would never do it again. The boat was getting to the end of its lifespan and was too small to deal with some of the strait's dangers.

The volunteers were nearing the middle of the strait when the call came through that they should head toward the diesel slick. They turned west. Ferguson leaned over the starboard side, trying to keep an eye out for anything. It was not an easy task – he did not even know how many people were missing. If there was someone out there in the water it would be the size of a football. That would have to be spotted while hurtling across the waves at 25 knots.

They had been travelling toward the slick only for a few minutes when Ferguson thought he heard something – a faint sound that made him turn his head. About 100 metres away, slightly behind them he saw it. It was after 6 p.m. and the sun had almost disappeared but Ferguson knew there was something out there. It was a flash of red. He told the skipper inside to move towards it. Then he locked his eyes, raised his finger to point and did not waver.

For years he had practised man overboard drills. He had helped recover bodies of those who drowned in the *Kotuku* tragedy. He was only 21 back then and the experience had fazed him. He was older now and he knew the job well. He would not drop his hand until the boat was right on its target.

His eyes were bloodshot. He looked cold. The target was shivering and nude. It took three of them to haul him aboard. His weight dropped onto the floor of the boat.

'Take me to the engine room,' Dallas Reedy said. It was 6.11 p.m.

He wanted to put himself against its warmth but there was no such room on the boat – just the two outboard motors. Instead, the skipper Bill Ryan took off his thermal suit and wrapped Reedy in it. They tried to wrench his grip from the petrol canister. It was clamped on. He did not want to let go.

Reedy could barely move. He was hypothermic but to his surprise he could still feel the cold. His body was not numb. Reedy was a master diver and had certificates in everything from body recovery to free diving. When he went hunting for shellfish he hardly ever wore a wetsuit – even in winter.

The volunteers started asking him questions: When did the boat go down? How long had he been out there? How many people were aboard?

Reedy could hardly speak. But from what they learned it was not sounding good. Did he see anyone else get off the boat? Reedy hadn't. But still, Ferguson thought, if they had found one alive, perhaps there were more.

'You are still hoping,' he said. 'But you know the chances of finding someone else alive is pretty slim. It's not very often the Foveaux will release everyone.'

Reedy was choppered to hospital by Chris Green, who had first sparked the search. Police organised the fishing vessels into position. They lined up in parallel lines. The coastguard was at either edge to maintain structure.

The Rescue Coordination Centre, based out of Wellington, organised the pattern using data like the winds and tides. As more information was gathered and more debris found the search area tightened.

At 8.30 p.m., the first body was found.

The navy ship HMNZS *Resolution* was on its way to a training exercise in Fiordland, about 150 kilometres away, when it heard an emergency signal come over its VHF radio. Lieutenant-Commander Matt Wray responded: 'We are on our way.'

It arrived at about 11 p.m. Taking police and coastguard staff on board, it formed the centre line of a nine-strong search fleet scouring the darkness. Crew members used searchlights and sonar equipment to detect objects beneath the water.

An oar was found at 12.19 a.m., a blue duffel bag was found at 3 a.m. At 4 a.m. the search was suspended but the *Resolution*, accompanied by Bluff fishing boat the *Awesome*, carried on searching through the night.

By 8 a.m. the *Resolution*'s sonar had found what appeared to be a hull. It was 40 metres deep and lying on its side. *Awesome*'s crew lowered a camera down and confirmed it was the capsized boat.

A navy dive team was deployed from Auckland in a Hercules aircraft. They took with them specialist dive equipment and a portable decompression chamber.

At 12.45 another body was found. There was no lifejacket. Another was found ten minutes later. Again, no lifejacket.

The navy dive team entered the water and dove down to the boat. They traced the outline of the hull – the words EASY RIDER clearly visible through the turquoise murk. The life raft was still on board. A mattress was jammed against the wheelhouse door. The divers pushed it aside but the whole boat was empty except for a single, little black lifejacket. It was Odin's. The emergency beacon was still flashing.

The legacy

The pāua shell lay on a coffee table in an Invercargill home. It was surrounded by photos – of Boe Gilles, Shane Topi, John Karetai, Paul Fowler-Karetai and his son Odin. Rewai

Karetai was there too – all staring out from the frames. The ashes of Peter Bloxham were at the front, a mesh All Blacks cap hanging off a small white box. His wife Marama still had not scattered them. She did not know where to put them. She thought about taking him back to the Muttonbirds but maybe she wanted him close. She was meant to go back to the islands this year but felt it was not the same anymore. Boe, Peter and John would go every season. Now the place felt different.

She and dozens of other family members had been at Bluff's shore during the search, waiting for good news. But as it dripped in it became clearer. Aside from Dallas, the only one not related, none of them were coming home alive.

Dave Fowler was never found. Odin was never found. Paul was never found. Rewai Karetai was never found.

It had been almost two months since a judge imposed a fine of more than $200,000 on Gloria Davis and the company that owned the *Easy Rider*. It was ruled she caused or permitted the *Easy Rider* to be operated in a manner causing 'unnecessary danger or risk' to people on board and that as a director of the company which owned the boat she 'acquiesced or participated' in the failure of that company to take all steps to ensure that no worker was harmed aboard the boat. She was also convicted of operating the *Easy Rider* knowing a skipper's certificate was required and not held.

Gloria dabbed her eyes with a tissue as the victim impact statements, all of which supported her, were read to the court. Families of the deceased had not wanted reparation, so no order was made, Judge John Strettell said.

Davis told the court she accepted her responsibility but was 'too emotional' to say anything else. She stepped outside the Invercargill courthouse, took a breath and made a statement.

'When you have no control over the farm or the boat or the business, you should really remove yourself from the director role.'

For Marama, the case had brought it all back. Peter was not meant to be on the *Easy Rider*. He was supposed to leave with her the following week. Her children were going to join him but they decided not to. There were still so many questions. How long were they in the water? Were they in pain?

The questions weighed on Rhys Ferguson too. It was pure luck they found Dallas Reedy. If they had been told to head straight to the diesel slick then they would not have seen him. But if they had done something different could they have saved more?

When Gloria walked from the court feelings were mixed. Hadn't she suffered enough? Why punish her even more? But still, others said, she had broken the law and justice had to be seen to be done.

And already there were signs the *Easy Rider*'s legacy would not be forgotten. It was the largest search and rescue operation in Southland. There were 240 hours of helicopter flying time, 15,000 man hours and almost $400,000 spent by police. If the fishermen and volunteers had billed for their petrol that number could have been close to $1 million, district police commander Inspector Lane Todd said.

It was the greatest loss of life at sea since the 1968 *Wahine* disaster where a ferry capsized near Wellington killing 53 people.

Andy Johnson, the coastguard president, said people were more strict with lifejackets now. Especially with children. The trip to the Tītī Islands would continue to be made, he said. People just needed to make sure lessons were learned.

'Everyone still remembers the tragedy and the trauma and

the loss,' he said. 'It stays with you. Hopefully that will keep the pressure on that we need to be more and more careful.'

There had been talk of a memorial to those who died on the *Easy Rider*. For a time friends and family wanted something to go at Stirling Point at the far tip of Bluff where the road ends and the water begins. But then, after some conversations, a new idea was born. The coastguard boat that plucked Dallas Reedy from the water was old. There had been fundraising for a new, modern-designed boat for years. It was agreed – the funds should go towards that. It would be a living, working memorial to them. It would be on the ocean. It would help save lives.

Two months later Dallas Reedy goes back. He has been to hospital and heard people call his story a miracle. He has appeared on television and been in magazines. Now it is quiet and he wants to see the boat once again. It is 40 metres below the ocean.

He glides through the wheelhouse and into the cabin. It is bare. Everything has been sucked off the walls – clocks that were screwed on, lashings around the handrails. Drawers empty. The ocean has stripped it clean. He swims outside, pulls out his knife and thinks about making his mark. Perhaps his initials: D T R. Then he digs the knife's tip into the hull. He carves a simple message: 'Dallas was here.'

On his left arm is a tattoo. It starts at his wrist and flows up to the image of a Māori warrior on his shoulder. Boe Gilles did much of the work. He left a gap on his forearm. For a long time Dallas did not know what to put there. The day he came out of hospital a tribute to those who were lost was inked into the empty space.

Helicopters still shock him. The sound of outboard motors still jog his memory. He still keeps the petrol can in his bedroom. He still calls it Wilson.

Even now, more than two years later, he will wake at 12.03 a.m. – the time when the wave hit. Six months ago he awoke to see the dark outlines of all those who were lost on the *Easy Rider*. They surrounded his bed. He looked around and saw all of their shapes, all of their heights. They did not scare him. He thought they must be worried about him. Then he went back to sleep.

His story is now his family's story. He wants his sons to know what he went through and what he did to come back to them. He wants them to know the blood that runs through his veins is theirs too – Ngāti Porou – warrior blood.

He is does not believe himself to be an exceptional person but now understands that if you push yourself exceptional things can be done. His initials are D T R – Dallas Tuamoana Reedy. Tuamoana: 'He who stands steadfast in the sea.'

Ali Ikram
Beyond the Headland:
An Encounter with Keri Hulme

Out beyond the headland, the strait is grey-black. The rolling swell hits the bow of the ferry, each time producing a towering cascade of salt water. The *Santa Regina* is nearing the end of her service life. A steady ship – ideal for traversing back and forth between Wellington and Picton. This is mild. It gets much worse. Sometimes you can't stand up. 'I've seen three hundred people all lying on the floor clutching sick bags,' the woman from the ferry company's marketing department says. The words offer only a mild form of reassurance. Either way, I would still quite like to vomit. I turn off my microphone, retreat to the bridge's small office and begin clearing a box of paper in preparation. A series of folk cures are offered including sucking an ice cube, all to no avail.

Tangaroa, the sea, is not my element, though my travelling companion on this northward odyssey is quite taken with it. Keri Hulme lives six months of the year by the ocean at Ōkārito on the West Coast in an octagonal house; the rest of the year she is based in Ōamaru to be close to her mother. A fifth of a life spent watching the Tasman roll in. That is, if it's not between September and mid-November, when the 67-year-old will be in the surf holding a long-handled net scooping up inspiration. For whitebait holds a cherished

First published on 22 May 2014 on The Ruminator: ruminator.co.nz place in her oeuvre: the thousands of juvenile galaxiids are a wriggling, translucent, ink-eyed muse.

An hour below decks honking your stomach contents into small bags in a ferry cafeteria reserved for long-haul truck drivers gives you time to think. Between the violent convulsions, there is an impossible stillness as unexpectedly sudden as the bile. Enough time to wonder – if this isn't your element, what is?

'Keri says this is going to be her last public appearance and her last TV interview. It's a major. I think it would be great for John Campbell to do it. It really requires someone of his stature. I think Keri would feel better about doing it if he was involved,' said the book festival publicist. Unfortunately – for everyone – he was not available and so the task fell to me. Two days prior to the blighted crossing I had thrust the copy of *the bone people* purchased at the university bookshop at Canterbury twenty years ago into my pack and boarded a flight from Auckland to Christchurch. There I was joined by camera operator Jabulani Ndebele for the drive south to Ōamaru. Keri Hulme does not travel by plane; she does not fear flying, but avoids this mode of transport because of lung infections picked up mid-air. The idea was that we would accompany her on parts of the 1324-kilometre journey by land and sea to attend the 2014 Auckland Writer's Festival, while interviewing her along the way.

'You have been recognised by one of the staff behind the bar,' said the waitress at Robbie's Bar and Bistro in Ashburton, where Jabulani and I had broken the drive south to have dinner. 'Can you please sign the menu?' Now it hangs next to a picture of my beaming face, beside other luminaries who have passed through town and stopped there, including the World Champions of Robotic Milking. 'Going to Oamaru to interview Keri Hulme,' I wrote next to the signature, hoping it might prop up any claim to notoriety. 'Who is she?' enquired the waitress.

That night when we pulled into Ōamaru, the grand lime-stone buildings glistened like teeth, white and wet. Little blue penguins scuttled away from our headlights as the car drove over the cobbles in the historic quarter. In many ways, my journalism career had begun on the main street, with a horrendous two-week secondment to the local paper. It all started promisingly with the front-page lead on an accident with a hedge-trimming machine which flung a large macro-carpa branch through a family's front window. A photo of the lank-haired son holding the offending chunk of wood and looking mournful heralded my arrival as a coming man. But my later mishandling of another big story (on the opening of a second-hand electronic goods store) led the editor to dub the fortnight a bit of a disaster. 'Normally, when students do work experience with us we take their names and call them if a job comes up. I don't know whether we should do that with you,' said the paper's manager. 'It will be interesting to see where you turn up,' were his words in parting.

Fifteen years later, I had returned.

Television is my element, if it may be classed as one. It is highly unnatural, though. Neither water, air, fire nor earth, but as ubiquitous – a layer superimposed on the physical world. We take existence, cut out the pauses, stillness, and frequent boredom, and sell advertising in the spaces left behind. It is easy to forget how turbulent this flow of life can be until it mingles with another more rarefied current.

So it was on a Wednesday morning in Ōamaru, I – a denizen of this fallen world – came face to face with a true artist. So bold and uncompromising is Hulme's vision that the author took sixteen years to write her first novel and so far three decades completing the next. The yeti has made more media appearances.

If you are going to conduct a rare interview with a notoriously reclusive famously cantankerous writer my advice is: don't be late. And, if you are late: don't be sixteen minutes late. There was a legitimate excuse. The railway crossing in Ōamaru had malfunctioned, causing a traffic jam that we eventually avoided only by driving on the wrong side of the road around the barrier arm while I stood on the tracks watching for signs of an oncoming train. The excuse, however, cut no ice.

When I arrived on the doorstep, one I had travelled quite a long way to stand on, I felt as dejected, lost and initially unwelcome as Simon Gillayley, the mute, tousled boy who washes up at the tower of one Kerewin Holmes in the author's magnum opus. The door was thrown open by an unseen hand to reveal Hulme on the phone, remonstrating with the director of the writer's festival, adamant the interview with me was not going to happen. 'She's pissed off,' observed Jabulani as Hulme stormed up the garden path towards the road where she carried on loading her van. In her defence, the writer did say she had emailed the festival to cancel the interview the night before. Perhaps the message hadn't made it through, or perhaps the wheels were so well in motion by that stage it was thought best just to allow us to work it out face to face. It is beyond question that we were late, and because of her poor eyesight Hulme must drive during the hours of daylight, which would have added to the anxiety caused by our tardiness. Either way, psychically, I rolled into a ball and began deodorising the air with an apology every ten seconds.

Then Keri stopped dead – it felt like a final line was about to be delivered, before we were left standing on a damp pavement watching the van drive away. 'Do you realise you have arrived among a family of cannibals?' she demanded. 'We were famous for eating each other during feuds!'

We all have ancestors squatting on our shoulders and in that moment of challenge I felt one of mine stirring. It was my late paternal grandmother, a Rajput from the warlike clans of northern India. 'Come home with your opponent on your shield or dead on your opponent's shield,' was the way their women would farewell their men in wartime, and when the battle was lost those men would take off their armour and charge to meet death wearing only saffron shirts, and those women would throw themselves from the battlements.

'Well,' I replied. 'I am Pakistani, and we know a thing or two about feuds. A relative once spilled acid on my grandmother's face during a feud over money. She spent years undergoing plastic surgery – when the science was in its infancy – to restore her appearance. This was after she killed a cobra with the single blow of a broom.' Perhaps it was thanks to this tale of a formidable matriarch, but somehow I found myself in the van with the author and we were on our way.

From the doorstep, as Keri had paced about, I caught a glimpse of her own mother in the background. Mary is one of the unsung heroes of New Zealand literature. She raised six children alone after her husband died when Keri, the eldest, was aged eleven. Mary refused to believe there was anything wrong with her child when teachers judged Keri to have a learning disability; indeed, the problem was an inability to read the blackboard due to problems seeing it. Mary nurtured her daughter, who was obviously different – as a twelve-year-old, retreating to bed to read Kipling with a candle under the blanket. Mary was the only person allowed to suggest changes to *the bone people* after it had been rejected by every publisher in Australasia. When Keri won the Booker Prize, she sent the cheque to Mary. And it is Mary who has been promised that *Bait*, the long-awaited manuscript, will be finished by the end of the whitebaiting season.

It is a little-known fact that before becoming the country's best-known literary recluse, Keri was a director on *Country Calendar*. So she is well versed in the technical requirements of a TV crew. Even accounting for this, and the thaw in relations, interviewing her was a cross-country scramble. Jabulani managed to mount a GoPro on the dashboard at the petrol station in Ōamaru, but before he could strap his camera into the back seat to record the audio of our conversation, she drove off with only me on board. I had to do my best to capture what was said on a cellphone. At one point Hulme explained that the reason she did not pursue a longer career in television came down to the fact she found many of the people involved in making it to be fake. Only by Waimate did she remain stationary long enough for us to be wired for sound.

In Timaru, we parted company, the first leg of the journey complete, with a plan to meet again the next day in Picton before boarding the ferry. I had asked to be dropped off in Christchurch, but Keri is reluctant to go back to her home town after the earthquakes. I unburdened myself to my producer, Pip Keane, who consoled me that at least it went better than when John Sellwood interviewed Janet Frame: 'At first she wouldn't let him in the house and spoke through a crack in the door.' In fact, Frame wouldn't come out till John played the bagpipes outside her window. But such an initial reception from a brilliant loner doesn't mean they don't like you. John ended up playing the pipes again, this time at the literary great's funeral. A character in her final scene.

The next morning a panicked call came through from the festival publicist asking if I knew where the great author was, as that night she had not slept in the Picton hotel the festival organisers had arranged. The news that Keri Hulme had been spotted at a fish and chip shop in town prompted jubilation. Good camera operators have a set of instincts that are honed around the timely delivery of a quality finished product. On news of the sighting Jabulani erected his tripod down the other end of the street from the chippie and set the camera to a long lens. The question: would our unpredictable subject cooperate today, or would the only thing we salvaged be the blurry sequence of a Booker Prize winner striding purposefully towards us with a couple of pieces of blue cod and half a scoop under her arm?

Believe it or not, though, even journalists on the hunt have a conscience. I recall asking myself in that precise instant the one question reporters in my field ask most often but seldom aloud: 'Why are we doing this, again?' Television crews only set up a shot like this for two reasons: when the subject is under surveillance and has done something wrong, or when making a nature documentary on an endangered species. While in this case our quarry was certainly not the former, it is quite possible she was – in a way – the latter, the possessor of original thought.

Eventually, Jabulani took down his tripod and packed up the camera.

David Fisher
The OIA Arms Race

Good afternoon everyone. I am David Fisher, a reporter with the *New Zealand Herald*. I have worked as a journalist for 25 years, mainly in New Zealand but across a number of other countries.

I think there's some value before I start in placing a context around the current situation in relation to the media and the Official Information Act.

In doing so, it should be said each of the following allegations is denied.

At the moment, there is an inquiry under way into whether a blogger gained some advantage in receiving information from the SIS for political purposes. There are allegations of preferential treatment over the OIA involving the same blogger and the former justice minister.

The police are also facing allegations of trying to cover up juked stats by burying an OIA. And a former Customs lawyer has said his organisation preferred to let requests languish in the Ombudsman's office rather than dealing with them.

In the 25 years I have worked as a journalist, there have never been so many questions, or such a loss of faith, all at once.

First given as a speech to an audience of public officials in Wellington on 15 October 2014 and subsequently published on Public Address: publicaddress.net; and the website of the *New Zealand Herald*: nzherald.co.nz

So, when thinking of the OIA, I had thought to start in happier times.

The difference between when I started 25 years ago and now is astounding when it comes to dealing with the public service. If I was writing a story then which in any way touched on the public's interaction with government, I would pick up the phone and ring an official. It really was that easy.

Receptionists would direct you to areas in departments, and staff there would know who would be best placed to fill the gaps in my knowledge. That's what we in the media need – knowledge. We don't need quotes, although they inevitably come with the information. We need information, unvarnished, unspun and in a form in which we can understand what it actually means.

When I started, if I wanted to know about something, I would ring and ask. For example, if I want to know about how kauri stumps were exported, I would ring up the equivalent of the MPI – Ministry for Primary Industries – and ask how kauri stumps get exported. I would then spend half an hour on the phone to the guy who oversaw the exporting – often the guy who was physically down at the docks – and I would be informed.

It seems a novel idea now. I can barely convey to you now what a wonderful feeling that is, to be a man with a question the public wants answering connecting with the public servant who has the information.

I remember exactly when I sent my first OIA request. It was in 1993 to a crown health enterprise, the structure which managed health at the time. I remember why I turned to the OIA. There was a communications manager there who was difficult, obstructive. He was risk averse, complicated in his evasiveness. He was, in short, ahead of his time. In a decade many others would be as he was then. And, in a decade, this communications manager would be working for a giant tobacco company.

When I returned from working in the United Kingdom, in 2002, I found the public service still open and accessible but there were many more communications managers than there had been previously.

Then, it was the flow of communication they tried to manage – not the content or nature or it.

And this is how it worked. I would ring up to find out about exportation of kauri stumps. Reception would ask where I was from and, hearing I was from the media, would put me on to the communications department. The comms person there would listen closely and then go away and work out who had the answers for me. When they found the right person, that person would ring me – or I would be given their number to ring them.

Interviews would happen, which they generally do not now, and they would typically be about the most mundane matters. How does government work? Explain the machinery to me? And what came out the end?

It was process stuff – because, basically, that's what we do. We find out how the world works, and we explain it to our readers.

I would speak with those who were able to explain the machinery to me. Having taken that on board, if it worked – then it worked. If it didn't, then it didn't. There was very little spin. It was a lot more honest than what it became.

It was, when you think about it, the OIA in action. My questions were verbal requests and the responses were the official information coming back.

The shift really began after the 2005 election, when Helen Clark's third term threatened to get away from her. I believe what happened then perverted all that has come since, when it comes to media and the public service.

The 'no surprises' policy had been a feature of coalition agreements since 1996, and part of the state-owned enterprise model.

It did what it said on the box – meant there would be no surprises for the government. Initially, it was a safety valve put into an agreement – a chance for someone to ask, is it a good idea to sell half of Transpower without telling the prime minister? Big things. Really big.

But before long, it crept out of SOEs and political agreements and spread its grip through the public service.

Ministers realised they had a device through which they could reduce the surprises they suffered. And, as it went on, the surprises ministers no longer wanted to experience became greater in number and smaller in significance.

Increasingly, it placed on the public service a political imperative which it had never had to shoulder. It had to think about what it might be that would surprise a minister. Decisions were made with the minister's discomfort in mind. Decisions were being made which were political in nature.

The answer to the question 'What would surprise a minister?' is pretty much anything. Damned journalists, you never know what they're going to do with information. Best not to give them any.

Interviews became fewer. Comms staff became distant and difficult.

Suddenly, to get information about how kauri stumps were exported, I went from ringing and asking and interviewing to ringing and then being told to put my request in writing.

The email would zip off and I would sit and wait. I know now, from the sources I have developed inside public agencies, that people would look at those questions and wonder what I was really after. A day later, I would get an email back answering my questions in the most unhelpful way you might imagine. They are cowardly answers, with a flinch in every sentence, as if they might be surrendering the nugget I was really after – apparently the tool I can use to undo the machinery of government and bring it all crashing down.

What I would be sent were lines to fill a hole. There's an impression among some that we need 'talent', or lines in a story – like a hole in a wall needs Polyfilla. The 'lines' would arrive at 5 p.m., as the person who sent them to me ran out the door.

Such idiocy.

Now, the interviews are gone. We speak to public servants when they have something really good to boast about, or really bad to apologise for. There is no in between. We meet only at weddings and funerals, and that's no way to build a relationship.

The rest of the time, we don't really know what the other party is doing. We still need information, so we find other ways to get it.

Increasingly, as interviews fell away, we would send OIA requests. The less you spoke to us, the more we asked for. When civility was gone, we turned to the law and expected that to give us the answers we needed. I send more than a hundred every year.

Gradually, we began to suspect we were being screwed in this way as well. Ministers don't like being surprised by anything. OIA requests would be processed – then sent to the Beehive for sign off. I have the flow charts. I see the processes. They require OIAs which are being sent to the media to be sent to the minister for sign off first. It astonishes me that any minister would think they have any business reviewing OIAs before they get sent out.

Before long, it seemed nobody wanted to surprise the minister. I've been told of officials deciding to remove surprising material before it went to the Beehive.

I know of ministers who have received the results of mundane requests, going through the 'sign off' process but sending the OIA late because they are hunched over the response searching for 'what that bastard Fisher is really after'.

Where does that leave us?

In a dark place. I have a fairly combative relationship with many in the public service, largely because of the type of story I do. I was concerned I had a view which was too dark, too harsh, so I canvassed widely among colleagues before coming here. I was wrong.

There are far darker, grimmer views out there than mine. Simply, we don't trust you. By commission or omission, we think many of those who handle our OIA requests don't have the public interest at heart. We don't trust the responses we get.

Of course, we may be completely wrong. We may have made a terrible mistake. But how would we know otherwise? You don't talk to us anymore. You're too scared to. Caught between the Beehive and the media, you don't know which to face.

Or at least, that's the impression we have.

And again, we might be completely wrong.

The publication of *Dirty Politics* told us much of what we thought we knew. The examples in there are from ministerial offices – but they are so familiar to what we experience from government departments.

I spoke with a public service staff member in the four months before the election to ask after an OIA. She said to me, 'I'm really sorry, you're not getting as much as you normally would because the election is really close.'

I have had OIAs stalled in the run-up to the election.

If anything, they are meant to come faster. But the two months leading in to the election were a drought. Since September 20, it's been chucking it down. Right now, long-delayed OIAs are turning up on a daily basis.

Or they are not. A colleague of mine came to see me yesterday. 'Have you given your talk yet?' he wanted to know. 'I've got to get this off my chest.'

There was a report he had sought which existed in a 'draft' form until the minister's signature made it final. The OIA was filed months ago, the delaying tactics used to push it off. The response sent to the reporter gave an express written assurance that, when it was signed off, it would be released.

The election came and went. The reporter has chased it up, only to be told there will be a 'general dump' of information in a few weeks or a month or so. The report will be released then, among that material, buried in a mass of information.

If you think about how that happened, it can be matched up with the law. The delay for another twenty working days, the extension for consultation, then the indefinite put-off because the information is going to be released publicly.

But it's not the spirit of the law.

The 'general dump', or the soon-to-be-released-publicly, is a good example of what we see as evasions, and how we develop workarounds. Again, I say these are what we as media see. The public service might see it differently.

The general dump started to emerge a few years ago. They push off release of information outside the timeliness of the news. Rather than talking about an issue within the time-frame in which the event is happening, it gets shunted out into the future where it is less relevant. It comes, usually, late in the day, often late in the week. Thousands of pages of material dumped online. Always dumped in a form that cannot be text-searched.

Now, there may be a perception among those who handle these things that it's a good way to bury bad news. That's what we think you're doing. The number of people who will trawl through documentation looking for that single line, or match facts over long timelines, is relatively few.

It turns into a bizarre arms race.

We now use amazing analytical tools. They will take scanned PDFs and turn them into a searchable format. What's more, they will categorise, timeline, entity-match characters, dates and other players throughout the thousands and thousands of pages. It becomes a library of information which we revisit time and again.

The Ministry of Business, Innovation and Employment has gifted me such a tool with the SkyCity dump. When I got a tip a few weeks back that the SkyCity contract had changed, I could search every document publicly released and build a timeline of every reference which had been made to identify the change.

The other workarounds we are turning to are much worse than technology-enabled journalism. Sources have always been a key part of what I do, what journalists do. They are more important than ever now. I find myself talking to people about taking photographs of documents with their iPhones, sending me pictures of papers so I know what exists when I'm asking for it. I'm often less interested in getting what I've already got than I am in seeing what gets withheld.

I talk to public servants about copying papers, getting thumbdrives on to work systems, uploading files on to cloud servers – and how to do it without getting caught.

When I turned to my colleagues about this, I asked a range of questions, but there are three which really matter, because they are based on the three guiding principles of the legislation.

Does the way the public service handles your requests achieve the following: a) Enable more effective participation by the public in the making and administration of laws and policies? *Sometimes.* b) Promote the accountability of ministers of the Crown and officials? *No.* c) Enhance respect for the law and promote the good government of New Zealand? *No.*

A very experienced political journalist told me:

> The whole culture of the Wellington public service towards the OIA is governed by two things – the need not to embarrass your minister or your department (putting your chances of promotion or even your job at risk) and the need to uphold the law, which public servants are more conscious of than you might think. The result is that public servants block requests for as long as they can and delete as much as they can using whatever section of the OIA that they can.

I'll tell you an exception, or an example of doing it right. It is not an exception which governs the entire agency, because there's always headquarters. There are about 9000 uniformed police staff. They are all in a position where their general orders mean they are able to respond to questions from the media on issues in which they are involved.

Police comms staff can be difficult like any other government department – although I personally think they are better.

But with so many public-facing staff, there is an acceptance staff will speak. Trying to stop them all from speaking on matters in which they are involved would be like trying to catch rain drops.

The best advertisement the police have is a constable or sergeant telling the public what they did for a living that day.

It's openness, honesty and having the courage to back your staff on the job.

It's not always possible when the Beehive comes calling.

It's 2014 – thirty years since the OIA began working in practice, 32 years since it was passed.

There is so much that we ask for which is public service core business, it's hard to understand why it is not classified at the point the information is created.

Surely after thirty years of dealing with largely the same type of information, it should be known what can be withheld and what can be released.

There should be no surprises, for anyone.

Nicky Hager
Loose Lips

On 2 October 2014, five detectives and a police computer expert spent ten and a half hours raiding my home. They took all of the phones, computers, hard drives, USB keys, CDs and other electronic devices, as well as an assortment of files.

They were trying to uncover the identity of a confidential source who had given me information for my recently published book about New Zealand politics. The book had revealed a campaign of dirty tricks being run out of the prime minister's office, including an organised system for smears on political opponents.

But I'm sleeping easy; I'm as certain as I can be that the raid was a waste of the police's time. It won't help them at all to find my source.

This is an issue vexing investigative journalists around the world: how to protect sensitive sources in the era of widespread surveillance technologies. I have heard a lot of pessimism about how it is no longer possible to keep confidential sources safe – sources here meaning whistleblowers and people who leak important public-interest information. I don't agree. Investigative journalism is as possible and powerful as ever. I believe that if we understand the risks and do our job properly, we can continue to protect our sources, as I was able to do with the sources for my recent book.

I love the work of investigative journalism. For people with

First published in *Overland* 219, Winter 2015: overland.org.au the right aptitude and motivation, it is one of the most socially useful things they can do. I want to share with you a sense of what this work is, how it is done and why it is so worth doing. But first I want to start with the subject of protecting sources in the digital age.

The first thing the police looked for when they arrived at my house – the first thing they always look for – was my mobile phone; they were rather crestfallen to learn that I do not use one. (I know this is unusual, but in my work I prefer mental space to immediate availability.) Mobile phones are pretty much self-surveillance devices for people who have things they need to keep confidential. They are also one of the main ways that police investigate crimes: by seizing a phone, the police instantly get an alphabetised list of friends and associates, piles of text messages with dates and times of activities, often a GPS record of your movements, photos with embedded times and locations, and more.

Over the years I have written quite a lot about police and intelligence, and so I understand many aspects of how investigations are handled. I certainly don't believe the NSA and satellites track me wherever I go or anything like that. They don't. But whether you're a shoplifter or a whistleblower, mobile phones are the most likely way you will be traced. For this reason anyone with a sensitive source should never use their phone to contact said source.

You may have heard stories of the lengths people will go to avoid interception, such as removing the batteries from their mobiles or sticking them in the fridge. In truth, most people who imagine they are being spied on are worrying for nothing. But if there is a serious need to be careful, such as protecting a sensitive source, people just shouldn't use mobiles. Leave them at home – it's as simple as that.

The main reason is metadata, that word that firmly entered the modern vernacular with Edward Snowden. In practice, the police do not bug many phones. It takes too many resources to listen to and transcribe spoken conversations, and so the practice is generally reserved for serious crimes. But 'call data' or metadata – easy and readily available – is the police's investigative tool of choice. Call data includes the records of who you called, when you called and the location of the nearest cellphone tower. The same databases that save this data also save all text messages to and from your phone. In New Zealand, this data is automatically saved for all mobile phones for three to four months; in Australia, courtesy of the recent amendments to the Telecommunications (Interception and Access) Act, this data will be stored for at least two years. The police routinely phone or email the telcos and get this information to help their investigations.

The solution to this is awareness. We shouldn't meet a confidential source in a busy café and, likewise, we shouldn't leave great big digital footprints between ourselves and our precious and vulnerable sources. Many sources are caught, particularly in government agencies, because the agency owns and stores all its phone logs. When there is a leak investigation, they can do obvious checks such as any incoming or outgoing calls from the journalist who did the story. We just need to understand the risks and, when it matters, never leave electronic tracks.

So how do I contact sources or potential sources? Usually it's a face-to-face encounter, or sometimes I call from an untraceable phone. After that it's at prearranged meetings set up the last time we saw each other. Sometimes high-tech, but usually simple and low-tech. I do not encrypt my email or waste time worrying about surveillance for 99.9 per cent of my communications – but I do make sure I am very careful when it is needed.

The next thing the police looked for in my house were any computers. My main computer, like many people's, contains mountains of emails plotting my life hour by hour. But I have always made sure there were no tracks to the source of my book. (Incidentally, deleting something on most computers doesn't remove it entirely.)

Even in the unlucky event that the police win the current court case and are granted access to my computer, they will find that the hard drive is encrypted and has a nice long password. A six- or seven-letter password can be cracked in quite a short time by a simple computer program that tries a, aa, ab, aaa, aab and so on. Thus, each additional symbol in a password makes it much harder to crack.

I am not a computer whiz. For such tasks I seek out very experienced IT people to help with things like computer encryption. I find that collaboration between investigative journalists and IT whizzes is a very productive matching of skills.

I should add that the kind of precautions I'm talking about here aren't needed for most situations. I don't think countries like Australia and New Zealand have armies of secret police taking an unhealthy interest in everything we do. Indeed, I spend my life reassuring people that they really don't need to worry about being under personal surveillance. But sometimes we do need to take it seriously – for example, when it comes to protecting confidential sources.

The most important protections are the basic pre-digital ones, in particular knowing how to keep a secret. Not being able to do this is, in fact, the biggest risk.

Many people cannot keep a secret. Secrets create an irresistible urge to share. If we 'just tell one person', they are likely to tell someone else who cares even less about keeping the secret and – by natural laws of physics – the news accelerates outwards.

I say to sources: 'We need to put a fence around the two of us and never tell anyone else what we're doing for the rest of our lives.' It is simple and effective. It means there are some marvellous stories that can't be told, but there is no alternative. Part of a journalist–source relationship is being there to give care and support to your source, especially early on when they are feeling vulnerable. In most cases, the people who have helped me reveal big stories seem to feel pride and satisfaction in what they have achieved. Often a special life-long bond is formed.

The final step in protecting sources is the care needed when writing the story. The facts that we know and those that we don't know can be like a great big arrow pointing at a few people as possible informants, and so it is vital that great care is taken in how this information is presented. The specialists brought in to study a government or corporate leak go first for the organisational call data – logs of who accessed which documents and so on. Next, they study what details are in the story, which have been omitted, what years the information covers, which staff know what bits of information and thus, by triangulation, who their suspects are.

Once we understand this, we can take precautions. I picture a security officer studying a leak, and go to great effort selecting what information to include, what to leave out, where to supplement from other sources and, generally, how to bewilder those trying to narrow down where the leak came from. I often find that, as I write, I am putting as much thought into what I might give away about my sources as to what I am writing. This faithfulness to sources is part of my job.

If we are careful and do all of these things, I genuinely believe we can continue to get new sources and keep them safe.

I feel confident that sources such as the one the police were hoping to identify in the raid on my house will be just fine.

What I am saying is this: we can still work with sources to hold powerful people to account and to inform the public on big issues – and keep them safe in the process.

This leads to the big question: why? Why should journalists and sources risk themselves for the sake of a story? What purpose does investigative journalism serve?

Daily news is reasonably good at reporting what 'newsmakers' say and do in public, and blogs and commentators are good – sometimes very good – at discussing and analysing that news. But the media system is weak when things are hidden, spun or manipulated – in other words, when it relies on press releases or other controlled messaging. It's a weakness that becomes apparent as soon as there are organised vested interests that have the resources and motivation to try to control information reaching the public, or to spin a preferred version of truth.

Investigative journalism is the activity of unearthing and publicising things that challenge dominant views: finding out who is telling the truth, exposing unethical behaviour or dishonesty, giving a voice to people and issues that are hidden or ignored, digging deep on behalf of the public so that people don't have to live in a political soup of spin and half-truth. It is about providing a counter-narrative to that of the powerful.

It's not easy work, but it can be highly satisfying and worthwhile.

In recent years there have been some stunning, world-changing leaks, notably those inspired by WikiLeaks. Those leaks will undoubtedly lead to more people deciding to make important disclosures of a similar scale. But although there are similarities, that kind of leaking is not the same thing as investigative journalism.

Sometimes I wonder if those stunning revelations and information dumps have made it seem as if leaks just turn up on their own; perhaps giving the impression that investigative journalism is about setting up a secure cloud account on the internet and waiting for the leaks to come to you.

The heart of investigative journalism – and when I enjoy it most – is when you decide a subject needs investigating and set about digging down into the roots of the issue. It is a very strategic activity: studying a subject and then searching for the right investigative tools and sources to make progress. Personally, I have many subjects that I feel need work (and that are on 'the list') and I continue to search gradually for the right sources and breakthroughs.

When I start such an investigation, I make a 'map' of what sorts of things I want to find out about a subject and include all the possible sources (people and otherwise) that might help. I draw up lists of places where I would like to find insiders and make a register of fieldwork to be done, letters to write, experts to ask, overseas parallels to research and so on. Sometimes it's like a game or puzzle: I'm trying to solve a problem, find a missing clue. Often, because I am working on subjects that are secretive or intentionally hidden, I am looking for insiders and sensitive material.

And then, usually, a kind of magic occurs. I find that if I have bothered to think through what I'm trying to find, and brainstormed the types of sources I am looking for, they tend to come along. I unexpectedly meet someone who can help, or hear about a source of information that might be useful. Somehow, perhaps because I was on the lookout, the break-through happens.

This has worked for me so many times now – my first book in 1996 was about New Zealand's role in the Five Eyes intelligence network, and others followed on the military in Afghanistan, anti-environmental public relations and the inner workings of governments and political parties – that I have come to realise that if I do the work, I have a good chance of getting results.

But it's not really magic – indeed, some of my subjects haven't worked out at all yet. It is really a combination of planning, luck and then hard work.

Most inside sources who have helped me would never dream of being a Chelsea Manning or Edward Snowden. It would not even occur to them, or at least not seriously, to approach a journalist and become a whistleblower. Partly, this is why the secure dropbox is not enough. The vast majority of sources help because I have sought them out and asked. I have been able to reassure them that there is value in publicising the issue and that they can trust me not to get them into trouble.

That is my secret method: asking.

It is hugely important that potential sources continue to feel comfortable saying yes, and that there are journalists who keep seeking them out and asking for information. Many of the terrible issues in the world rely on secrecy; control of information and selected release of spin are part of how bad things can happen in relatively democratic and law-based countries. Insiders are often the only realistic way of getting information about hidden things. If people in power believe they can get away with keeping their actions classified, they generally act much worse than if they risk finding their grubby business or lies suddenly exposed on the front page.

But having willing sources is only half of the equation. One of the challenges for investigative journalism is not having enough people to seek out potential sources. And who is going to do that kind of work in increasingly stripped down and precarious news organisations?

I think we need to recognise that investigative journalism isn't just a speciality within the journalism field. Much of the best investigative work is done by filmmakers, authors and public-interest researchers, people who might not see themselves as traditional journalists but who are still fulfilling this critical role. It is a role in society defined by its goals, tools, methods and motivations, not by job descriptions and university qualifications.

Countries don't need hundreds of investigative journalists, but they need some – and the more the better! Every issue and every part of society that has decent investigative journalism is better off than the many areas that have no scrutiny. I have been part of international networks of investigative journalists for the last twenty or so years. Country by country, there are people who have done inspiring pieces of public-interest research that have helped to change the world.

Take, for instance, the Swedish TV journalist Fredrik Laurin, who felt suspicious when reading a government statement about deporting two men to Egypt in the early years of the so-called War on Terror. The government said that it had an assurance from the Egyptian government that the men would not be tortured, which is like an assurance from soft drink companies that they care about obesity. He went back to the film footage he'd taken of the aircraft taking off and found the aircraft's tail number, N379P. By searching on the net he found a story about the same plane collecting hooded detainees from an airfield in Pakistan, further spurring his curiosity. He followed this with letters to plane spotters around the world, asking about more sightings of the plane, which was registered to a US company with no office or staff, only an address in a legal office. Step by careful step, he and colleagues gradually uncovered one of the really important stories of that era: the CIA's 'rendition' flights, which were used to grab suspects from around the world and illegally move them to secret detention centres or Guantanamo Bay.

It makes me happy to know that people like Fredrik exist. We have worked together on other projects since then.

Similarly, one evening when I was in Switzerland, I had dinner with a South African investigative journalist named Justin Arenstein. He told me a story about an investigation he had conducted into vicious vigilante teams set up by white farmers to intimidate and punish black farm workers. He had moved into a rural area, ostensibly to look after a friend's farm for a few months, and it wasn't long before his neighbours encouraged him to do his bit to enforce their version of justice. Set up with hidden cameras, he went out on hair-raising night-time drives to sort out – that is, threaten and assault – the black workers. When Arenstein's exposé eventually came out, the country was shocked; the vigilante numbers decreased and the authorities were forced to stop secretly supporting them.

There are many more such stories. There is the Indian journalist catching corrupt politicians, the Mozambique journalist exposing illegal rainforest logging, others publicising unsafe factories all over the world or illegal fishing or countless other subjects. These journalists often make a profound difference to the problem they are reporting on: they uncover it, thereby stopping it being invisible or hidden.

The ones I respect the most are those who have kept going through the decades, continuing to uncover big stories and resisting the urge to be cynical or discouraged. It is always easier to decide that the world is a mess and that nothing can be done about it. In every era through history there is plenty of bad and depressing news to justify thinking the future is hopeless. But society has nonetheless made progress, and each era is much better than it would have been because people continue to be shocked and offended by injustice and inhumanity. And, crucially, some people do something about that.

Finally, there is a related 'occupation' that is worth mentioning. It is for people who work in governments, companies, political parties, PR firms and all sorts of other places, in senior or junior roles, who come across information of public interest and decide to tip off or pass those details on to people like me. You may one day find yourself in that position, as part of your career, or in a job you take to earn money for a while. If you find things that offend you and that the public has a right to know, then – with suitable care and thought – you can maybe do some good by working with a trustworthy investigative journalist to get that story told.

That is what happened with the main source for my last book – the one the police were looking for and, all going well, will never find. They did New Zealand a massive service by helping to expose the activities of the dirtiest prime minister in our lifetimes.

Ashleigh Young
Window Seat

At 8.20 on Thursday morning I found my seat, the middle of the row near the back of the plane, sat down, and switched on my Kindle. I was reading *The Examined Life*, Stephen Grosz's account of his experiences as a psychoanalyst, and I had reached the last section, 'Leaving', in which Grosz has taken on a new patient, a young man, who has just been diagnosed with HIV. The young man is beginning to spend all of his psychoanalysis sessions in deep, still, heavy silence, sometimes even falling asleep. I was at the part where Grosz is describing the different kinds of silences that patients sometimes bring to him – silences of refusal, or discomfort, of repression – when a tiny withered woman with a huge puffy black bag over her shoulder indicated she had the window seat beside me. I got up and helped her manoeuvre her bag into the overhead compartment, then she sat down and set about making herself comfortable; she took off her shoes, revealing papery brown feet, and arranged a blanket beneath her seat so that her feet had a resting place – her legs, in leopard-print leggings, were too short to reach the floor. She took out her own Kindle, which was in a proper zippered case, and I went back to Grosz and the young man in the therapy room. 'Under ordinary circumstances,' Grosz was saying, 'I might ask a patient who has been silent for some time what they're thinking or feeling,

First published on 9 November 2014 on Ashleigh's blog Eyelash Roaming: eyelashroaming.com and once or twice I did this with Anthony. But I soon realised that my speaking was an intrusion, a disturbance.' I stopped reading then because I couldn't focus. I was getting a sense of slight but building pressure between the window-seat woman and myself – a sense that she was about to say something; that she wasn't really going to read; she was just fiddling with the device while she decided where she would start with me. Sure enough:

'If you see me popping pills or dragging on an inhaler, don't you worry.' She had a bright Queensland accent, with an unexpected burr, almost Scottish-sounding. '*Bronchiectasis*. Much worse than asthma. Had it for years and years, so I've got all these scars on my lungs. Big knotty scars. Bronchiectasis. Last time I left New Zealand I took this sickness with me, now I'm going to give the bloody thing back!' She motioned at her tiny chest. 'I've had about a hundred pneumonias and a fair few operations. It was all the mould in New Zealand. That's why I moved away to Australia. But I'm tough. Don't worry if you see me puffing away.'

She looked at me sideways. She had blue eyes in a small tanned face, and one of those open-mouthed smiles that made it look as though she was silently saying 'Aaah!' She pulled a plastic lunch container out of the front seat pocket, cracked open the lid and took out an egg sandwich, which she ate while swinging her feet and looking out the window. We were right above the wing. Outside on the tarmac an electric cart was shuttling about, a hi-vis figure at the wheel. 'Sometimes when you're between New Zealand and Australia,' she said between mouthfuls, 'if you look down you can see a rainbow circle in the sea. A glassy sort of rainbow, like a big bowl. I always get the window seat so I can see it, because it's beautiful. But we won't be able to see it with that darn wing there.' I said it was a shame about the wing, and she said, 'No, not a shame, it's just the way it's happened.'

She was quiet for a while, and in the meantime an elderly woman sat down in the aisle seat, to my left. She had white-blue hair and was dressed in shimmery black clothing, with bronzer on her cheekbones and scarlet lipstick. She had the look of a dulled but beautiful gemstone, which seemed obvious even as I thought it, but I couldn't discard the impression. An opal, probably. (As I was thinking about what sort of gemstone she'd be I remembered how in Brisbane I'd thought aloud that the crows had eyes that looked like sequins. My friend James had said, 'Maybe the eyes have evolved to look like sequins, because crows know that humans like the look of sequins.') I helped the opal woman to adjust the direction of the tiny fan above us so that it was blowing directly into her hair, then we sat down. I was probably a frustrating barrier between the two women, making it less likely that they would talk to each other, when they might have more to say to each other – but then a middle-aged woman came down the aisle and handed the opal woman a packet of jellybeans. 'You'll need these for energy, Mum.' Her mother tucked the jellybeans away and reclined her seat and put her sleeping mask on.

'Last time I flew, I got terrible altitude sickness,' window-seat woman whispered. 'It was years ago. I remember lying on the floor under the seats thinking I might be dying. Suddenly the word 'God' came to me. 'God, God, God, God.' I felt like the word was beaming into me right down the centre, like a torch beam, filling me with the word 'God', and I thought, well, if this is dying, it's all right.' That must have been incredibly stressful, I said, and she jutted her chin upwards, squinting. 'It's how it happened, and it got me to where I needed to be.'

She looked out at the wing. 'This is the first time I've flown in many, many years.' The Scottish burr again. 'I haven't been able to, with my sickness. But if I make it this time, it's a sign I'll be able to make it to Switzerland, where my son lives. This is my test flight, you see.' She gave the *Aaaah* smile again. 'I'm meeting my sister in Wellington. First time I've seen her in five years. We were born in Invercargill. I had to leave because of the mould.' Then she told me about the first time she'd been up in a plane, when she was sixteen. Her friend's father was a pilot, and he had a small plane. They all went up together in the small plane and did acrobatics for half an hour. 'Straight after the flight, my friend and I went off to a dance. All dressed up in our miniskirts. I was feeling so sick. My very first dance, I vomited all over my partner! He was very annoyed with me.'

We were still on the tarmac, and I was already feeling tired, because I'd had to react with surprise and delight at these stories. My energy for talking to strangers gets quickly depleted. Maybe sitting next to window-seat woman would be too much. But she was quiet now, and soon we were in the air, and Brisbane, with its pale sky and all its evenly tanned people in sunglasses and sleeveless tops, was dropping away. Window-seat woman nudged me and said, 'Look.' She had something in her hand. It was a white rock with corrugated, granular swirls in it, the swirls like the movements of a worm or a centipede. It looked like it could be a fossil, but I couldn't tell of what. 'I couldn't resist picking this up on the beach early this morning. Nature! I don't suppose they'll let me through with it.' I started to laugh. I said I didn't think they would let her through with the rock. 'Well, it's here now,' she said, and put it back in her bag with satisfaction.

I had been up since quarter to five because I'd had to walk to the train station, with James, who was flying back to

Darwin. I closed my eyes and fell into a blank doze. When I opened them again I felt heavy and sad. I always feel a bit sad on flights between countries. I can't help thinking about the past and the future and where I will end up. The geographical limbo seems to emphasise a limbo I feel in myself. I was staring into space, thinking about all this, when the woman said, 'My brother's a cross dresser,' and I was jolted back into our little row. 'Been doing it for ten years, and has never been happier,' she said. 'He'd always felt pulled in all directions as a young man – he just wasn't ever himself. What grief. Imagine it. And when he was fifty, he met this wonderful woman who told him to just let go. Just let it out. And he started dressing like a woman, these lovely skirts, colourful shoes, and he and this woman who'd told him to do it, they ended up married. It was a real eye opener for our whole family. We all loved him but now we had to learn how to love him as a lady, too.' I got the sense she'd told the story numerous times but that she liked to tell it because it confirmed something she'd long believed. 'It's an amazing way to have your whole world opened up, you know – to have your brother or son or father say, I'm Harris, but I'm also Paris.' She prised another sandwich from her plastic container and began to eat. We were flying over the clouds now.

The opal woman took off her mask, shakily stood, and made her way towards the toilets, clasping one seat at a time in a kind of rowing motion. I stood up too, and the window-seat woman followed. Ordinarily I would've felt irritated, but I didn't with this woman. She didn't seem needy or searching with her stories, the way some fellow passengers are. She didn't seem to expect anything from me. We queued together at the end of the aisle, while the people in the toilets took what seemed like a very long time. Window-seat woman looked at me incredulously. 'Funny how some people take so long. Just like life, isn't it?' Then she looked fixedly at me and said:

'About forty years ago my brother – not the cross-dresser one, the other one – was flying over Saudi Arabia, and the plane got hijacked. It was in the days when it was easy to hijack a plane. The hijackers made the pilots land in a desert.' The thought crossed my mind that window-seat woman must be lying, at least exaggerating. 'They had to stay there for two days until they were rescued. My brother was fine in the end, and no one was killed. But he came back to us very much older.' She gave a strange sad laugh. 'And later on he ended up dying of AIDS. What a mystery.' A toilet door finally opened and she went in while I stayed waiting in the aisle. I thought about the book I had been reading and the young man lying silently on the couch in the psychoanalyst's office. It had taken Grosz a long time to understand that all Anthony needed was not to feel alone. He didn't need to talk, but he wanted to fall asleep without fear, knowing that when he was gone, he stayed present and alive in the mind of another.

Back in our seats, it wasn't long before window-seat woman spoke again, and for the next twenty minutes she told me that she'd once been a biker in the Hells Angels – had probably been one of New Zealand's first female bikers – but had got in trouble with the police so had to give it up; that she'd been thrown out of numerous nightclubs as a young-ster because her skirt was too short; that once she went to an auction at Lyall Bay and her young daughter had tripped over in front of her, and when she reached out to pick her up she made a particular motion that made the auctioneer think she was bidding, and she ended up buying a big oak table. She told me that it was in Lower Hutt when her real life began, because it was here that she realised she was a healer. A friend had arrived after a long flight and he had hurt his elbow lifting a heavy suitcase, so she put her hands on his elbow to comfort him. 'I felt this strange, powerful tingling in my hands and arms, and I thought I must be getting pins and needles. After a few moments I had this strong feeling that my friend's elbow was better now. I took my hands away, and he said, 'Gosh, my elbow feels much better.' I said to myself, 'I'm a healer, I'm a healer!' She said that many years later, she ended up with her own healing practice in Zurich. Her husband earned all the money, so she didn't charge for her healing services.

It was possible that she was recklessly inventing. Who easier to tell an imagined life to than a stranger on a plane whom you'll likely never see again? The geography and timescale of her life was erratic – she had mentioned Invercargill, suburbs around Wellington, Paekākāriki, all over Europe, all over Australia – and it was hard to figure out who she was without being able to connect her firmly to one particular place. The past seemed so vivid to her that it was also hard for me to grasp that some of the stories she was telling took place more than forty years ago. I made my mind up to not decide there and then whether she was telling the truth. I wanted to stay open for as long as I could. I was wide awake when she said, with resolve: 'Now, I'm going to tell you about you.' She had not expressed any particular interest in me until this point, beyond asking me how old I was and what I did for a living.

Opal woman was having a close, whispered conversation with her daughter, who had come down the aisle again holding a miniature hairbrush.

'You love your cat,' window-seat woman said, 'you love your cat very much, and you love all animals,' and then I realised that she must think she had psychic abilities, along with healing abilities. There was nothing to do but play along; I was trapped here. I told her she was right about the cat and the animals. 'You're very gentle,' she went on. 'At your core you are very gentle, though you can be spiky on the outside.' How does one disagree? Isn't that the basic human condition? 'Where do you live . . . I'm seeing you living on the top of a hill. Steep hill. And you're zipping about on the roads, very quick, very zippy. An explorer.' She motioned with her hands. 'You're very like your mother but you think she talks too much. Your father is a bit hazy to me.' She frowned for a while. 'You have more of a connection with one of your brothers than the other one, perhaps.' Then she shook her head. 'I could go on and on, but it wouldn't do either of us any good.' She laughed and said: 'I will just say, I don't see any black marks ahead. Isn't that great!' She peered at me. 'I also will just say, you need to clean your glasses.'

We spent some time in quiet. I tried to read my book again. Anthony had not died – in fact, after being told he might have two years left and that essentially he had no future, he had lived for a very long time. 'I now think that Anthony's silences expressed different things at different times,' Grosz was saying. 'Sorrow, a desire to be close to me but stay separate, and a wish to stop time.' Anthony was still alive at the chapter's close, and then I began a new chapter, about a woman named Alice P., who was trying to grieve for a baby she had lost but wasn't able to.

We were ten minutes from landing when window-seat woman turned to me and said, 'I wanted to save this till the very end. I see some big changes ahead for you. Your life is going to go like *that*.' She made a zigzaggy motion with her hand. 'Yes, you've spent so much time putting others first, and it's your turn now.' She looked at me with such kindness that I put aside, for a moment, the knowledge that this is what psychics routinely tell their charges, because this is what people want to hear. Everyone wants to feel chosen. Being told 'it's your turn now' feels like being praised, or needed, or pursued. But then she said, drily: 'I don't suppose you've met the love of your life.' I was flustered and felt a surge of annoyance. It was her knowingness, and her flippancy. I told her, 'I'm not sure I believe in that expression "love of your life". But I feel that maybe I have, actually, back home.' She said, 'Well, let's see. You're at the perfect age. Women come right at your age. Men never really come right.' I got really annoyed then – maybe she would go on to ask someone else if they had found the love of their life, and that person would grow doubtful about all of their decisions and throw everything away – and turned on my Kindle and read that Grosz's sister had been to speak to a clairvoyant when she had lost her home and all her possessions in a brush fire in California, in 2008. Grosz's sister says that through the clairvoyant she spoke to her and Grosz's mother, who had been dead for more than twenty years, and Grosz is surprised to find himself tearful. 'What did Mom say?'

We were descending quickly into Wellington now and I could see the hills and buildings taking on their familiar edges. The pilot had announced that the local temperature was 12 degrees, with a strong southerly making it feel colder than that, and a shriek had gone up from all the Queenslanders on board. I finished my book, and found myself crying. Window-seat woman murmured, 'Jerry must be missing you.' Jerry is the name of my cat. She said, 'Is that his name? Jerry? He'll be glad to see you.' I managed to say, 'Yes, yes it is,' even as I was shaking my head. At some point I must have said

Jerry's name to her, *I must have*, but as I combed carefully back through our conversation, I was sure I hadn't.

After we landed and were waiting for the seatbelt sign to turn off, she said to me, 'Do they still call Wellington the City of Angels? They always said that the angels help planes to get down safely to the ground.' I said no, I was sure they had never called it that. Then I helped her to pull her bag from the overhead compartment and a few minutes later she was swallowed by the steadily moving line of passengers ahead of me.

Vicki Anderson
Diary of a Christchurch Bus Passenger

I am the passenger and I ride and I ride. I stay under Metro Bus Service glass. I look through my window so bright and I see the city's ripped back sides, I see the bright and hollow sky . . .

30 March 2015: Central Station, Lichfield Street, sometime around 6 p.m.

Headphones in, my mind elsewhere, I don't see the young Polynesian man carrying the nearly empty bottle of vodka until he is practically sitting on me. I rip my headphones out as his thighs hit mine. The strains of a Chet Faker song spills from my headphones. 'Hey lady,' he says. I shuffle to the left so our thighs are no longer in contact.

A bitter wind whistles through the temporary bus shelter. He begins to cry. It's ugly crying. He hiccups and snorts. Snot dribbles down his face and he tries to wipe it away on a bare arm. Slurring, he tells me that his mum has died. A few hundred metres away a man is in the sky, looking down on us, as he pilots a crane.

I offer a tissue and ask if he needs me to call a family member or friend to come pick him up. His bloodshot eyes scan my face. 'Fuck you bitch,' he shouts. Placing the vodka bottle beside him, he lurches to his feet and sways from side to side, mirroring the load on the crane in front of us, before sitting down again.

First published in *The Press*, 30 May 2015.

Smacking his hands together loudly he turns to face me, and places an arm around my shoulders. 'Smack,' he repeats. 'I killed her with the car.'

A security guard appears and the drunken man gathers up his vodka and moves on.

'It's only Monday night.' The guard sighs. Another man mimes what looks to be some sort of sexual act in front of me before my bus finally arrives. I get off the bus at the Riccarton Mall stop. It is there, at 8.20 p.m., that my final bus arrives. I get home at 8.40 p.m.

A two-hour trip to get home is often the case since the changes to the timetable were introduced last December and the buses became colour coded, like The Wiggles, into Yellow, Blue, and Purple etc. Anecdotally, every fellow passenger I've spoken to in recent months has been greatly inconvenienced by these changes.

6 April 2015: Early evening and the sun is setting over Hagley Park

He is twelve or thirteen, travelling with his grandmother who doesn't speak English. At the stop near Christchurch Hospital he helps his gran on to the bus with one hand gently under her elbow and places $10 down.

'Whaddya want me to do with that?' the driver barks. 'I would like a fare to Riccarton for myself and my grandmother,' the boy says politely and clearly. The driver sighs. 'What did you say?' he asks. The boy repeats himself. The grandmother's gestures become more animated. She appears confused. The driver replies exaggeratedly slowly: 'Can you speak English?'

The boy begins to blush and shuffles his squash racquet from one hand to another. The grandmother waves her hands around and speaks in her native language to the boy who pats her arm gently with reassurance. The boy repeats that he would like a fare for himself and his grandmother. The driver looks down the bus at us, the other two passengers on board, and says: 'I'm sorry for the hold-up everyone, this boy can't speak English and I don't know what he wants.'

I call to the driver: 'He told you in perfect English that he wants to get on the bus with his grandmother, and he gave you the money to do so, can't you do your job?' The driver mutters to himself but hands the boy and his grandmother their tickets. Part-way through the journey there's a driver change-over.

The driver tells the newcomer that he's sorry he's late but had trouble with 'difficult foreigners'. When I get off the bus the boy catches my eye and gives me a small, thin smile.

7 May 2015: 5.20 p.m., Riccarton Road on the Yellow Line bus (The horror! The horror!)

All of the seats are full, people are standing in the aisle nearly to the back of the bus, but one man has greedily kept two seats to himself. He stretches his right arm across the back of the empty seat, like someone on a first date at the movies. A passenger taps his shoulder and indicates that he should give up this seat to a woman standing beside him. The man shrugs and does not move or offer the seat.

The rest of us, the huddled, steaming mass of humanity and smells and shopping and briefcases and small children wanting juice 'right now' standing in the aisle, stuck in bumper-to-bumper peak-hour traffic, exchange shocked glances at his blatant rudeness.

When my headphone straps break, a cool twenty-something bloke with piercings and a strange underwear-to-trouser ratio (how long will this underwear outside the pants thing last?)

hands me his left earbud. On it I listen to Drake. We become Facebook friends.

It's this sense of community among bus users that I enjoy. Generally we are not on the 'loser cruiser' because we want to be. Mostly we are a) too young to drive, b) too old to drive, c) can't afford to drive or d) have a health problem that prevents us from driving. We are the inconvenienced ones who stand in the cold together in solidarity for hours waiting to travel badly.

That said there are many positives to commuting by bus. It's a relatively cheap way to travel; in the mornings the bus smells like a perfumery of freshly showered delights; it's great to leave traffic navigation up to someone else and sit back and observe and contemplate the city and people-watch behind glass.

20 May 2015: 9.05 a.m.
As my bus pulls up to the stop I realise I don't have any coins. All I have is my last $20. I hand it to the driver. I apologise for not having the correct change. He looks up at me angrily. He makes a growling sound. It is a weird noise that makes me uncomfortable.

He thumps the $20 into his tin and says, 'This isn't good enough.' He growls again. I notice that he has unusually long yellow fingernails. A passenger seated behind the driver raises his eyebrows and smiles sympathetically. The driver growls again and dramatically produces three $5 notes and change. He throws the $5 notes towards the change receptacle but the door is open so they blow on to the floor and I have to scrabble around to pick them up before they blow away.

As he accelerates from the stop I tumble into my seat, bumping my knee on a metal bar. The man sitting in front of me smells like metallic cabbage. It makes me gag. I cover my nose with my sleeve. The shopping bag of the woman beside me spills on to my lap but she doesn't move it. I edge closer to the window.

In the short journey to Riccarton Mall, the driver angrily rides the accelerator, at one point driving over the top of a traffic island. Whenever he brakes suddenly we all lurch forward.

Talkback radio loudly blares on the bus stereo. The soundtrack to the driver's manic road skills is a woman telling the radio announcer that 'God owns our bodies'. Piously she recites psalm after psalm as our driver becomes more erratic. It feels like a movie scene. A movie that would star Samuel L. Jackson. I don't say thank you, as I usually do, to the driver at the end of the trip.

25 May 2015: A long, long time ago, in a city centre that seems far, far away from completion

In *The Press* and on breakfast TV a bloke from the CCDU comments on the opening of the new $53 million bus interchange. It opens a week later than planned after 'technical difficulties' but the occasion is described as the 'delivery of a major anchor project'. The second part of the building will not open for more than two months.

On social media bus users likened the building design to something from science fiction, saying: 'Thunderbird 2 could take off from that roof.' Another commuter notes: 'There's no sign of roofing yet and it was due to open yesterday – half a bus stop out of seventeen anchor projects?'

When I visit the new building and ask fellow passengers for their thoughts, most like the new building but the most common response is the underwhelming: 'At least it's warm.'

But, as Iggy Pop sang on *The Passenger*, 'everything was made for you and me, so let's take a ride and see what's mine'. Please ensure you have the correct change.

Kristen Ng
Hanzu in a Headscarf

'What are you doing here?' he asked with an authoritative bark of Putonghua. His AK-47-wielding comrade stood by, surveying the local bazaar as three-wheeled motor carts spluttered past with fresh-kill goat carcasses piled high on the back. I'd blatantly taken a photo of their armoured vehicle trucking through Kuche's Old Town.

'We are just travelling,' I replied sheepishly, lowering my head which was meekly covered by a blue and gold pashmina.

'Delete those photographs.'

I complied, with a machine-gun Mandarin stutter of 'sorrysorrysorry'.

'*Shēnfenzhèng* 身份证,' he commanded. The trisyllabic staccato has conditioned locals into producing their ID cards with the swiftness of a cat's paw.

'I'm a foreigner,' I conceded, as he took the black New Zealand passport from my sweaty palms.

Perplexed for a second, taking in my Han face, a foreign passport, a DSLR camera and a headscarf, he asked again, this time with a sense of curiosity intermingled with duty, '*What are you doing here?*'

One photo survived. A regular morning in Kuche کۇچار 库车, the first stop on my journey through the largest province in China.

First published on 8 June 2015 on Kiwese: kiwese.co.nz

Xinjiang شنجاك 新疆 is a mountainous, oil-rich region
that forms the bulbous bump of northwest China. Bordering
Tibet to the south, Mongolia to the east, Russia to the north
and with Kazakhstan, Kyrgyzstan, Tajikistan, Afghanistan,
Pakistan and India to the west, Xinjiang (which literally
means 'new frontier') has long been a vital trading hub and
cultural melting pot at the heart of the Central Asian Silk
Road.

Buddhism came and went; Islam came and stayed. Eurasian
peoples have migrated around the region's basins and deserts
for centuries. Xinjiang has been ruled by the Mongol Empire,
the Ming Dynasty and the Soviets, spent a blink as the Eastern
Turkestan Republic and, since 1949, has been under the
control of the People's Republic of China.

The Uighur نۇيغۇر 维族 (*Wéizú*) are the Turkic-speaking,
predominantly Muslim, Central Asian ethnic majority of
Xinjiang. However, it appears the government is working
towards diluting the Uighur majority by bringing more and
more Han Chinese 汉族 (*Hànzú*) to the region and imposing
restrictions on traditional Uighur culture, alongside efforts to
'现代化' (modernise) the area in line with the rest of the country.

In July 2009, violent riots in the Han-gentrified provincial
capital of Urumqi شەھرى نۇرۇمچى 乌鲁木齐 led to over
a hundred (Han) deaths, a temporary internet lockdown
in Xinjiang and the subsequent nationwide blockage of
Facebook, YouTube and Twitter. The car explosion at
Tiananmen Square and the knife attack at Kunming Railway
Station back in 2013 have both been attributed to Xinjiang
extremists.

Western reports on events in Xinjiang almost religiously
include the phrase 'ethnic tensions', while Chinese state
media tend to use the signifier '暴力恐怖分子' (terrorist), a

loanword for Islamic extremism inspired by the US response to 9/11. While variations on the word 'terror' including '反恐英雄' (counter-terrorist hero) and '恐怖训练营' (terrorist training camps) have been adopted by the likes of Xinhua and Sina, in Anglophone news reports their usage has been quarantined to inverted commas.

State media reports of Han death tolls and denunciations of Islamic (read: Uighur) separatists have created a fear-inducing, anti-Islamic mindset among the Han, many of whom receive their news through state media enclosed within the Great Firewall of China and hold a resolute distrust of the Uighur. Indeed, when my cellphone was stolen in Chengdu last year, nearby witnesses were quick to inform me that it was a 'Xinjiang man' on a motorbike.

Professor James A. Millward, author of the touchstone text *Eurasian Crossroads: A History of Xinjiang*, has suggested that the recent government crackdown on the defining characteristics of Uighur culture is the real reason for the unrest in Xinjiang and the spate of attacks on innocent civilians, rather than any militant jihadi threat.[*]

Even so, foreign media are often quick to hum the tune of the Chinese Government's heavy hand – the words to the song we all know. Anyone who has taken the most elementary class in Media Studies understands that the way in which the media report an event will influence the way we perceive it. With regard to ethnic tensions in Xinjiang, I think it's safe to say that people's perceptions have indeed been influenced. With this in mind, I covered my head with a scarf and tried to speak as much Uighur as I could during my trip.

---

[*] 'China's two problems with the Uyghurs', *Los Angeles Review of Books*, 14 May 2014.

I travelled to Xinjiang with Ben, a long-time friend from Wellington. Our chosen route was a ten-hour overnight train ride in the *shàngpù* 上铺 (upper bunks) out of Liuyuan near Dunhuang, the ancient Buddhist cave site and last major stop in Gansu. Ben and I were welcomed to Turpan تۇرپان 吐鲁番 with open arms – full-body, boob-patting, nutsack-tapping frisk-downs by gender-assigned security guards. Hellooo, Xinjiang! And as we travelled from the train station to Turpan City, a one-hour bus ride, we experienced at least three ID checks. The locals have to deal with these hassles with security on a daily basis.

The Chinese flag flew atop all kinds of structures, even a rickety shack with a teetering awning constructed entirely of old car parts. Beneath the colourful fabric sunshades of a Turpan food market we sweltered – all sorts of boiling, baking and frying was going on in steel pots over roaring, open flames. *Samsa* pastries filled with salty, tender beef. Fresh apple juice. Wonton soup and tea. 'WHISKEY!' claimed one juice vendor, pouring me a cup and thrusting it into my hands for the criminally low price of 1 kuai. Most snacks and beverages in Xinjiang linger around the 1-2-3 kuai mark, a steal compared to prices in the east.

'How do you say "thank you" in your language?' I asked the owner of the wonton stall, who was tending an enormous mound of spring onions with a cleaver. '*Raqmed!*' she replied with a warm smile. An enthusiastic woman nearby overheard our conversation and soon butted in. '*Raqmed! Raqmed!* Take my photo! And then take hers!'

Carpets, fabrics, patterns. A local guy approached us in broken English and said he cannot get a passport with a Xinjiang *hùkǒu* 户口 (registration). I'd later meet a habitually shirtless man with a Tibetan mantra inked across his back and a Xinjiang *hùkǒu* in his rucksack. He told me he couldn't even visit a scenic spot on the border with Pakistan in the province where he was born.

Later that evening, at a Famous in Turpan restaurant, the Uighur specialty dish 'big plate chicken' (*dà pán jī* 大盘鸡) emerged: two massive plates of spicy chicken, with flat noodles and potato. I finally understood why the waitress was baffled by my earlier request for rice.

'Welcome!' the laoban said in Putonghua, beaming from the neighbouring table. 'Where are you all from?' I responded, in a language that was native to neither of us, that we were from New Zealand, the Netherlands, France and the United States.

'Ahh, welcome!' he repeated, turning back to his table, then added: 'Just so you know, I don't mean any offence by asking.'

'Of course not!' I replied, and we shook hands and waved goodbye while saying '*bai bai*!' and the Uighur form, '*khosh*!'

Grapes are the main produce in Turpan. Though the town's predominantly Muslim population do not drink alcohol, we indulged in enough homemade red wine to take the edge off our late-night, high-speed and somewhat terrifying race back to the train station. Squashed together in the back seat, we met a portly Han businessman from Urumqi who was fluent in Uighur and Putonghua. Multiple languages chattered over the melodic Arabic scales and jangly rhythms of plucked lutes that blared from the stereo. Taxi music in Xinjiang is infinitely more enjoyable than taxi music in the rest of China.

High-speed trains have made their way to Xinjiang, and the line that runs through the belly from Urumqi to Kashgar has improved tremendously, said one Han driver from Gansu. I'd subconsciously begun to pronounce my '*sh*' sounds as '*s*', and he turned to ask whether I was from Sichuan. He'd been in

Xinjiang for more than 25 years, and likes it. After that long, he had learnt to understand Uighur, but there was only so much of the rapid, Turkic lingua franca that he could speak himself: '我的舌头发不出来 My tongue can't get the words out!' he said ruefully.

Chinese characters fell away as we moved further from the main roads surrounding the train station. Elegant hooks, calligraphic swoops and diamond-shaped dots of Uighur adorned the remaining dusty, flat brick buildings of Kuche's Old Town. Coloured headscarves for women and square, pointed *doppa* hats for men, white-grey beards on the elders. I felt impolite for trying to speak Mandarin in a restaurant where the menu was completely in Uighur for its Uighur-speaking customer base. Noodle soup and *nang* that tasted like pizza with a big pot of black tea, however, were achieved that morning. The locals quietly performed a small ritual prayer after their meals.

Big ornate doors opened into courtyards similar to those of the old Chinese courtyard homes (*sìhéyuàn* 四合院) to the east, which have now largely been bulldozed to make way for apartment buildings. The open doorways along one street, 热斯坦路 Rasta Lu, revealed all sorts of happenings: woodwork, noodles, dough, vegetables, toilet paper; barbers, dentists, bread makers, steel workers *tink-tink-tink*-ing away . . .

Nang flat breads sat outside the abundant bakeries, stacked and displayed with the same pride and precision as at Newtown New World. Bed bases covered with rugs for sitting and snoozing lay out on the street, occupied by smiling families and their gorgeous babies with big, wide eyes. The one-child policy does not apply to China's ethnic minorities.

A large clay oven revealed dozens of *samsa* stuck to the inner walls like lichen on a rock.

'*Samsa*,' I observed, sidling up to the beefy pastries to snap a photo.

'Mmm, *samsa*,' echoed a bystanding elder who wore the classic dark-green *doppa* hat, nodding with contentment.

Homeless old people with dark, leathery skin lined the bridge from the Old Town across the arid, scorched river bed; their hands outstretched with small wads of jiao notes, their toothless mouths wailing in a tormented arrangement of Uighur. Later that day, I saw an impoverished man sprawled on the ground of a food street, eating the fallen peanuts from a nearby stall.

Wandering around Kuche with our backpacks in the sun, we had the first of many encounters with Xinjiang ice-cream. A sweet, tangy concoction solidified in a rotating freeze machine and was scooped into little pottles of goodness for 1 kuai a pop. Armed cops sat idly among apples and water-melons. Vendors crouched next to their vegetables and bowls of yoghurt covered with white cloth. A three-wheeler trundled through the bazaar with a baby strapped into a hammock in the back.

A Uighur man jammed on his three-stringed snakeskin *satar* outside a neighbouring teahouse. His strumming wrist was sore, so he let me have a try. The instrument had a chunky neck with frets marked by fine, nylon string, and a twangy timbre similar to a Turkish *doshpuluur* I had played in Litang. The community gathered round with intrigue. An older lady plonked herself down and spoke with me at length in Uighur about an unknown topic. My awkward interjection – '不好意思, 我听不懂 Sorry, I don't understand' – did little to break the flow of her mystery monologue.

It was humbling to sit at that tea table with them – welcomed without question into the bosom of their community.

A bizarre remix of 'By the Rivers of Babylon' played on repeat with another random club banger on the 民族街 Food Street. Sweet potatoes, Turkish egg pancakes, lamb skewers, more *samsa* and ice-cream. We eventually found ourselves walking past a Uighur primary school as class was let out for the day. Kids spilled out on to the road, hopping on the back of mini motor-buses home. Boys played in water spouting from a burst pipe. Stuffing our backpacks with munchies for the train, we began the journey to our final stop.

In the southwestern city of Kashgar قەشقەر شەھرى 喀什, closer to Bishkek, Tashkent and Islamabad than to Beijing, we were greeted with security scans, black dogs and riot cops armed with rifles. On the bus into town, a Uighur was punched in the face by a Han. There was a brief scuffle, in which no one dared intervene.

In the half torn-down yet still majestic ruins of Kashgar's original Old Town, bulldozers sat on top of cleared land, and the omnipresent red Chinese slogan banners (横幅 *héngfú*) hung above. Daylight brightened the multilayered façade of stucco, stone and square edges, while at night the floodlights would cast dramatic shadows across its face. Random cows continued to graze and shuffle about on a street behind the construction site. Disembarking the bus, we clambered up stone stairs into a grove of alleyways, overpasses and balconies, all of which seemed eerily deserted except for a few remaining families. Two locals were casually torching severed goat heads in an open furnace. A woman tossed a bag of rubbish on to the crumbling ruins of a former neighbour's home.

The Pamir Youth Hostel sits next door to the Id Kah Mosque مەسچىتى ھېيتگاھ 艾提尕尔 in the centre of town. It is owned by Wu Laoban, a skinny, chain-smoking Han from Heilongjiang in the far northeast – a province famed for sub-zero winters, the Harbin Snow and Ice Sculpture Festival and year-round coal smog.

Wu is staunchly anti-Muslim and despises the Uighurs for despising him. He freely discussed them alongside the need for '控制' (*kòngzhì*), control. Once part of the majority, as a Han Xinjiang resident Wu had become one of the 少数民族, the ethnic minority. When I asked Wu if he could understand any Uighur after four years in the province, he shook his head vigorously and replied that he only knew the sound of the Uighur slur for 'fuck you'.

As an optimistic foreigner who had been in Xinjiang for all of five days, I told Wu about the positive experiences we'd had with the local Uighurs so far.

'Try going out alone,' Wu said, smoking another cigarette in his non-smoking hostel lounge, '*without* your foreign friend.'

It was as if he was daring me into some kind of imminent peril; and his words sent shivers down my sweat-ridden spine.

One evening, after a late Kashgar sunset on the hostel rooftop, where people were playing cards, eating fruit, and smoking cigarettes while sitting cross-legged on cushions atop the low wooden platforms draped with the psychedelic green, red and yellow teardrops of that quintessentially Xinjiang fabric, three geared-up cops with flashlight-mounted AK-47s swept through the door. Yikes! Was this a raid?

Once they'd gone, I asked Wu's girlfriend and co-laoban, known to all as 'Zhao Laoshi', what had just happened. Zhao Laoshi was tapping away on her cellphone, completely unfazed by this apparently routine procedure. Not even semi-automatic weaponry could thwart her unbroken round of Candy Crush. She said they get checked only occasionally, while the Uighur-run hotels get checked every night.

The call to prayer stirred me at dawn. Patting around for my glasses, I shuffled out the glass sliding door. Sunrise was brewing beneath the horizon, as if being slowly conjured forth by the warm, sonorous incantation from the mosque. I boiled the jug and steeped myself in the tea-leaves of early morning, while official Beijing time stood two hours ahead of the sun.

Later on, the public bus was chock-a-block with mostly Uighur school kids and locals heading home for lunch. My apparent 'husband' Ben was sardined up the aisle among the other commuters. A little girl of perhaps eight years old bravely posited a question to me on behalf of a dozen curious classmates.

'姐姐, 你是美国人吗? Big sister, are you American?' she asked in perfect Putonghua.

'不是, 我是新西兰人! No, I'm a New Zealander!' I replied, sparking a flourish of Uighur analysis among the throng of tiny children. The leader spoke again.

'姐姐, 你是汉族吗? Big sister, are you Han?'

'是的. Yes.'

This set off excitable chatter, accompanied by a headscarf gesture. Students are prohibited from wearing headscarves to school in Xinjiang. The resident Han tend to stick to the Han areas, and speak of the Uighur areas with caution and trepidation, in the spirit of Mufasa warning Simba against venturing into the shadow lands beyond Pride Rock.

A Han Chinese girl on board the local bus was unusual; and a Han Chinese girl wearing a headscarf was a delightful anomaly.

'*Bai bai*!' they chirped gleefully, full of waving and smiles as they bounced off the bus and into the street.

On the last Sunday of our trip in Xinjiang, I ventured out 'without my foreign friend' to test the strength of Wu's evaluation of Uighur–Han relations.

There's a kind of wide-eyed innocence and vulnerability that comes with being a non-native speaker. You have less suspicion of people, you are less jaded, you have less experience in traversing the markers of character through the nuances of speech.

Ordering food in Kashgar in Mandarin:

Me: 'Do you have noodles?'

Laoban: 'Yes, but not till 10 a.m.'

Me: 'Great, just another ten minutes!'

Laoban: 'No no no, 10 a.m. Xinjiang time!!'

Lamb for breakfast, again.

Tea was served first, in a white teapot inlaid with ornate turquoise flowers, followed by a bowl of *polo* پولو 抓饭, Uighur pilaf: a generous pile of rice with grated carrot and an unbelievably breakfast-sized lamb bone planted on top. A side platter of neatly arranged vinegary preserves, bright orange and yellow-green atop the washed out blues, purples and browns of the woven tablecloth. Breakfast for one. '*Raqmed*!'

The streets of Kashgar show their roots, a deep-seated tradition of trade that dates back to the travelling merchants of the Silk Road. Animal carcasses hung upside down from every third or fourth shop, carefully inspected, pinched and prodded by local consumers and restaurateurs, selected and chopped up on a wooden board with a small axe, *thwack-thwack-THWACK*! Salesmen proudly puffed and groomed their fur hats with a longhaired brush, spinning the dust off each one with the flick of a wrist. Burgundy beads and necklaces dangled from storefronts, while bloodied goat heads lay on the street corner with open eyes.

The Kashgar Livestock Market 动物市场 and the Sunday Market 星期日市场 are often considered 'must-sees' by tourist guidebooks, and I was eager to get lost in the madness alone.

With spot-on directions from Zhao Laoshi, I put on my head-scarf and was off. I caught the #7 and the #23 to the Livestock Market – the only visible foreigner on board either bus.

When the #23 rattled to a halt at the final destination, the driver yelled out the name in Uighur and a bearded elder in a dark-green *doppa* gestured to me that we'd arrived. I joined him on the human migration up the road towards the market entrance and he said something to me in Uighur, to which I apologetically uttered, '听不懂 I don't understand.' He calmly raised his right hand with a nod of acknowledgement, as if to flick away his passing comment with a wave goodbye.

My scribbled notes on the day are loose and frantic: 'absolutely bonkers, chaotic, manure, loud, wonderful, hot, gross, shocking and wow.' Trucks sped down the road, full of sheep with their heads clamped in a row. A man and a woman were cracking up as they tried to wrangle themselves on to a 50cc scooter with a live goat positioned sideways across the footwell, clearly seeing the utter ridiculousness of the situation.

Near a grassy embankment, a dead sheep was strung up by its hind legs and sliced down the belly with a knife, whereupon its pink-grey guts fell out of its body with the gravitational spill of an unzipped bag of toiletries. Further along the road, a donkey harnessed into a wooden swing structure had a back leg being slowly winched upwards with a pulley. Oh, whew – just a donkey shoe-repair station!

Goats, sheep, horses, camels, cows and people with hats and veils of all fashions, even more diverse than the ones seen in town, blurred into one manically bustling scene. Breeders from all over the region flock to this market every Sunday; the constant yelling of bargains in an incomprehensible (to me, anyhow) babble of Eurasian dialects underscored the constant mooing, baaing, neighing and whinnying.

I edged forward through the swine and legs and poo, behind (and at times almost beneath) a gridlock of livestock vehicles, horse-drawn carriages, colossal bulls and small children, garnering my fair share of stares and quizzical looks. Donkeys bucked about wildly and camels bared their big, yellow teeth. Carts sped off and sent cow dung flying into the air. The edges of the market were lined with tarpaulin-covered eateries, where fiery ovens pumped out *samsa*, noodle soups and endless pots of tea, as crowds of men in *doppa* hats sat around the clusters of tables. Herds of goats were pulled around by hollering businessmen. A horse rider galloped down the rocky mud-gravel at the back of the yards, creating a satisfyingly crunchy *cloppity-cloppity-CLOP!*

Bereft of company to verbally ping-pong my impressions off, I found myself gasping aloud into the hot stench of livestock and manure. Curious at everything, yet urged along by the overwhelming sense of movement, I kept shuffling through the endless stream of living, breathing things. Being encircled by a cart doing donkey doughnuts up and down the market strip was enough to make my heart rate spiral upwards. Despite all the staring, I felt slightly intimidated but never threatened – like a Chinese girl turning up for kapa haka practice, or a tomboy walking into Glassons.

Reaching the outer edge of the Livestock Market, where fruit and vegetable wagons were parked up, I was relieved to be around some non-sentient produce. Leafy green tobacco was rolled, curled and twisted into filter-less cigarillos by a wrinkled man with nimble fingers and a herd of customers. I stumbled out of the gates with bewilderment written all over my face. Two vendors called out to me and asked if I would take their photograph. The picture shows the two of them beaming big smiles alongside their truckload of watermelons.

I caught the #23 bus back into town, with locals packed in as tightly as goats in the back of a pick-up truck, to visit the Sunday Market. The roads were criss-crossed in all directions with motorbikes, buses, cars, pedicabs, horse-drawn carts, fruit vendors, snack trolleys, shoppers, pedestrians . . . pretty much anything with wheels or feet. Outside the Sunday Market, I bumped into some of the other Chinese crew from the hostel who were heading back to Id Kah. When I told the girl from Jiangsu that I'd caught the bus to the Livestock Market and back, she stared at me as if I were Joan of Arc, or Mulan.

Zhao Laoshi had mentioned there was a section out the back of the main shopping area where the locals go to shop. Out the back was indeed where the action was. Anything and everything was for sale in enormous quantities. Kid vendors shouting about shoes. Feeding-frenzy bargain bins. Trestle tables of torches, aisles of alarm clocks and of course endless stalls of patterned materials. There was some serious shopping going down. If the Livestock Market was a male domain, then the Sunday Market was 'where da ladies at'. Arabian-style white veils with regal crowns on top, high turbans, loose flowing veils, classic tied-back kerchiefs and more. Some women had drawn their eyebrows on with blue eyeliner in a straight line across both brows. I purchased a length of clashing red-yellow fabric, deftly cut and measured by a barefoot textile vendor.

I was exhausted, hungry and sweaty; it was time to retreat to Pamir. The roads were chaotic, the buses bursting at the seams. A three-wheeler with rug-covered benches on the back was chugging past while the driver yelled out 'ID KAAAAAAH!! ID KAAAAAAH!' so I flagged him down and hopped on, joining an ancient woman in a pink veil, a mother and daughter and a *doppa*-wearing elder. Six more people would squash in with us during our 3-kuai zip through the backstreets to the

Id Kah Mosque. Whizzing down these alleys I'd never have known about, past a guy kneading mud concrete with his bare feet, through the distinctive smell of cumin and spices from the charcoal-smoked lamb kebabs. People piled in as quickly as they piled out. At the mosque, the driver sped off and I was left standing alone in a plume of speeding cart dust.

'Huh? How'd you get back so fast?!' the Chinese crew asked a little later, surprised to find me back at Pamir before them, and chowing down on a freshly purchased serving of potato chickpea salad.

Because I trust the locals. Because I have trust.

Jenni Quilter
2WW

On the 28th of June 2015, a nurse rang me up and told me – in a conversation that lasted less than thirty seconds – that at the age of thirty-five, I had diminished ovarian reserve. This is exactly what it sounds like; I did not have the eggs I should have. Contrary to how I looked and felt, to statistical norms and inheritance patterns, one part of my body was ageing faster than the rest. My cupboard was bare.

I had expected to begin IVF (in-vitro fertilisation) that day. In the morning, I had gone into the clinic for an ultrasound and blood work. They saw eight follicles in my ovaries, which are the casings that eggs grow in; it wasn't a huge amount, but it wasn't terrible either. But my blood work said something else. My FSH (follicle-stimulating hormone) level was very high for my age, which meant that my body was already used to the hormones I was planning to inject myself with for IVF. My body wouldn't react; the follicles I had wouldn't be able to grow eggs en masse so that they could be retrieved two weeks later. My AMH (anti-Müllerian hormone) number was too low, which indicated I had very few eggs left. These numbers were more appropriate for a woman in her forties. But the nurse did not say all of this. She simply said that I could not begin IVF, and read out my FSH and AMH numbers. When I asked to talk to the doctor, she told me he would ring the next day. And then she hung up.

Written in August 2015 and first published in *Tell You What*, November 2015.

I had been lying on the couch when the nurse rang and for a minute or two, I didn't move. I thought about the medicine in my bedroom, which I had laid out on a bookshelf the day before; large packs of syringes and different gauge needles, vials and micro-fine injection pins, needle disposal containers, box after box of the different medicines. Some of it was stored in the fridge. The medicine had arrived earlier in the week in two large boxes, and cost approximately $8000. I was lucky to have good health insurance.

I had spent the previous two weeks preparing myself for the next two weeks. I had undergone an HSG (hysterosalpingography), which involved flushing irradiated water through my fallopian tubes and uterus and photographing the glowing lines of liquid to check for blockages. I had watched videos of how to administer the two to four injections I'd need every day. I knew how to use a Q-tip and diluent to turn a solid tablet of Menopur into an injectable liquid. I knew how to load a Follistim pen cartridge, how to set the dosage, how to pinch my stomach so there was a roll of flesh for the needle to enter. I had accepted the likely side effects, which included weight gain, bloating, cramping, mood swings and headaches. I knew I wouldn't be able to do yoga, or cycle, or even swim. Twisting the torso can damage the swollen ovaries – each of which can grow to be between the size of a lemon and a grapefruit. Now none of that mattered.

I walked over to the table and my laptop, and typed my FSH and AMH numbers into Google. This was one of the first paragraphs I read, from the Reproductive Medicine Associates of Michigan: 'Essentially, an elevated Day 3 FSH value indicates a very poor prognosis for conception through IVF and a high risk of pregnancy loss should the rare conception occur. Unfortunately, if you ever exhibit an elevated FSH value, having a normal value at a later time does not favorably change this prognosis . . . At RMA, we have determined that an FSH value of 15 or higher predicts that IVF will be of no value in helping to achieve pregnancy. FSH values over 14.5 have produced only rare pregnancies in our program.'

No *value*. My FSH was 14.3. (For most women my age, it is under 10.) The website went on to recommend egg donation, which is when you pay for another women's eggs to be fertilised, and then transferred to your uterus. My genetic line would end with me.

The knowledge of what a human egg looks like and how it functions is remarkably recent. This is partly because semen is so obvious. Aristotle thought semen gave women's 'matter' form, and most monotheistic religions considered semen the primary component in creation; women were the ground from which man's impulse might grow. In the second half of the seventeenth century, a group of Dutch and French scientists began to develop the hypothesis that if there were eggs in rabbits, insects and viviparous dogfish, there might be eggs in women. In 1672, Regnier de Graaf noticed that the follicles of rabbits reddened and ruptured following mating and three days after copulation, small spherical structures were found in the fallopian tubes. These scientists' dissections of women's bodies revealed the structure of ovaries and a uterus, though the men still could not find an egg. In 1674, a Dutch draper-turned-scientist called Antonie van Leeuwenhoek, using a single-lens microscope, looked at his own sperm and found hundreds of tiny 'animalcules' swimming in the liquid, but no one put two and two together and thought to use a microscope to look for eggs in a women's body for another one hundred and fifty years. It wasn't until 1827 that a human egg was actually spotted by a man called Karl Ernst von Baer.

I imagine these scientists in their houses, the corpses of animals and humans piled up in their laboratories: a Soutine painting pulsing with death. I wonder whether they had children, or what their wives thought. All of these discoveries, set against life itself: upstairs, an eleven-month-old who won't stop crying, who is teething, who happens to take more after his mother than his father. Downstairs, the scientist is sitting at his desk, drawing his findings, the fallopian tube opening into the uterus like a flower or canyon.

In 1866, the American surgeon J. Marion Sims published his clinical notes about women's fertility. He described how to carry out a digital exam and introduce a speculum, how to remove polyps ('they may be cut off by scissors' with perchloride to stop the bleeding) and how to deal with vesicovaginal fistula (a hole between the vagina and bladder that is caused by prolonged labour). He thought conception only happened during menstruation. The book, *Clinical Notes on Uterine Surgery: With Special Reference to the Management of the Sterile Condition*, is available online. You can still sense his scientific excitement, his sensitivity for his patients' embarrassment. He had an examination chair specially made (24 inches wide instead of 18, 30 inches high instead of 22) so that women could recline and remain upright. These patients were mostly white, and from money. (In this sense, the IVF game has not changed.) Sims had moved to New York from Alabama, where it is likely that he developed his surgical techniques by experimenting on African American women who were slaves.

In his book, Sims described one patient, 28 years old, who had been married for nine years. Sims tried to inseminate her for nearly a year. He did this at the Women's Hospital, which was located on Madison Avenue and 29th Street (a few blocks away from my own doctor's office). Approximately once a month she climbed into his chair, and her husband went into a room nearby to masturbate. My heart breaks a little at the tedium, the desire, and the grief. The couple finally fell pregnant, but in her fourth month the woman fell and miscarried. 'The mother recovered with the greatest difficulty,' Sims wrote. He did not try to inseminate her again.

I did not find these stories when I searched for my FSH and AMH numbers. Instead, I mostly found myself in fertility chat rooms and message boards; my search terms had snagged conversations between thousands of women, who shared protocols, advice and stories about their doctors, who commiserated with others' bad news and celebrated pregnancies. Many women had an automated signature, which contained an abbreviated history of their IVF journey. This is a typical one:

> Me 40 (just turned) DH 42 TTC 2 yrs
> Oct 2011-IUI #1: 1 folli – canceled :-(
> Nov 2011-IUI #2: 2 folli, HCG trigger, prog tablets = BFN
> Feb 2012-IUI #3: natural cycle, HCG trigger, insemination mistimed (thanks a lot) – BFN
> Apr 2012-IVF #1: Getting ready for IVF with donor egg – DE from sister who is 38 yrs, yikes! (it was all we were comfortable with, she is older but everything looks good – fingers crossed)
> May 29: 2 Embies . . . 2WW!
> BFN – wasn't meant to be

In other words, this was a 40-year-old woman, married to a 42-year-old man. They had been trying to conceive for two years. She had undergone three intrauterine inseminations (IUIs), likely stimulated by hormones. The first was cancelled because only one follicle developed and, presumably, the cost couldn't be justified. For the second insemination she had two follicles, and was given an hCG trigger shot (a massive dose of human chorionic gonadotropin that stimulates ovulation). She took progesterone tablets to develop her uterine lining so that an embryo could successfully implant, but nothing did. The third IUI went the same way, but they mistimed the insemination (there's a reasonably tight timeframe of 36 hours between an hCG shot and when an egg is released from the ovaries). Then she tried IVF with her sister's donated eggs. They succeeded in creating two embryos, which were transferred into her womb on May 29th. She waited two weeks, and got a BFN (a Big Fat Nothing), rather than a BFP (Big Fat Positive).

These signatures gave context. They functioned like the history of a word in a dictionary; whatever the specific issue or question this woman was responding to on the message board, you could follow her back in time, see how her infertility had evolved at a glance. These signatures were their accommodation with medical science, the notes they had taken for themselves. *This is what I've gone through, and this is how I'm going to tell it.*

I read about success stories. Many women pointed out that although FSH and AMH numbers predict egg quantity, they don't always predict egg quality, particularly in younger women. I could, it seemed, fall pregnant naturally. *All it takes is one good egg*, women wrote over and over again, acknowledging the truism, and pressing on nonetheless. *May your embie be sticky. Baby dust for everyone.* But I also read a lot of pain and disappointment. There were women who had been trying to conceive for more than a decade, who had gone through eight rounds of IVF, who had gained 30 pounds in hormonal weight. There were couples who had remortgaged their house to pay for the treatment, who had broken up. There were women who described the pain of a sister falling unexpectedly pregnant, or a friend who decided to have an abortion. There were women who could not bring themselves to go to the company picnic because as soon as their colleagues had a beer or two, they would ask her why she hadn't had kids yet and she would have to decide whether to be honest. On some of the message boards, you were expected to put at the top of your message if children or pregnancy were mentioned in the post below. Some women described not being able to leave the house. Their grief was deeper than mine, bigger and wilder than I knew how to bear. There was a country out of there of women lying on their couches in the afternoon, faces puffy with tears, bones grinding with a need they could not fulfil. *The only thing I ever wanted was a child*. I read that hundreds of times.

I had not thought to read these sites before. I was young; I was healthy. I had thought my decision to delay having kids was the only real impediment to falling pregnant.

And this is how I fell into the internet.

For the past fifteen years, I've spent at least four hours a day looking at a computer screen, but I had always bounced across the internet like a skipping stone, gathering information, unaware of my own momentum. Now, the internet became a whirlpool, a vast grey eye looking back at me, pulling me away from my interest in anything else. In the days after the nurse rang, I could not work. I could not write. I could not watch a movie or a television show. All I could do was read thousands of messages on these boards, clicking the hours away, allowing these women's words to pile up like sand in the corners of a room. For the next fortnight, I read thousands of pages, novels-worth of messages.

The doctor eventually rang, and sounded despondent. 'We can try to test again next month,' he said. 'We'll wait and see if your FSH goes down.' I could hear the doubt in his voice.

'Are there any supplements I can take?' I asked. I had read up on substances like DHEA and CoQ10.

'I don't think they work,' he said.

'Does stress raise FSH levels?'

'No. If anything, it probably depresses them.'

I kept on reading, and made an appointment for a second opinion from another doctor. I would have to wait until my next period when my FSH could be retested, and while I waited, I read until my eyes hurt, and still kept on. My path had forked. I could see myself in another life, injecting these drugs, going to work, seeing friends, but now I was surrounded by fog. I could observe, but couldn't act.

I had the strong sense of entering a fairy-tale. My body was a vast palace, and I had just discovered there was one room, tucked away, in which time had sped up. The furniture in there was light with age and the husks of insects. It was a secret I wanted to forget. A witch is not a woman with special powers. A witch is a woman who has lost her powers, who has to resort to spells and potions.

There is some evidence that acupuncture helps fertility, so I found a doctor in traditional Chinese medicine in midtown. Every Monday, I made the trip, and lay in one of eight tiny consultation rooms, waited on by her many smiling assistants.

Before they began the acupuncture, they cupped me, which involved lighting alcohol swabs inside small glass jars, then quickly attaching the cup to my lower back. The suction formed by the vacuum of oxygen draws blood to that area of the body. I was instructed to lie still on my stomach for ten minutes. If I moved at all, the glass knobs would shift and tinkle against each other. I felt like a fragile stegosaurus.

Then, after they'd pulled the cups off (with a delicious sucking noise), the doctor would come. She seemed to cycle endlessly through her consultation rooms, from woman to woman; ten women an hour, eight hours a day, six days a week. She would feel for my pulse with a hand as small as a child's, and ask me to stick out my tongue. 'Aaah,' she would say politely, and make a note in my chart in Chinese. I was drinking her bitter herbal tea twice a day.

'Better?' I'd ask.

'Yes,' she'd say.

Then with firm, quick movements, she'd insert the needles in my head, ear lobes, stomach, hands and legs. Tap tap. Tap tap. 'Meditate on your womb,' she'd say, then turn the light off, leaving me alone for thirty minutes. I frequently fell asleep.

Sometimes, as they removed the last of the needles, the assistants would stroke my hair, giving me a tiny caress that nearly always moved me to tears.

I was told that I was yin deficient, that I shouldn't do yoga in a hot room anymore, that I needed to slow down a little. I tried. I did not think it was going to work, but her treatment gave me a semblance of control; here was something I could do.

In 1968, an American couple called Doris and John Del Zio married. Though both had children by previous marriages, Doris couldn't seem to fall pregnant, and they were referred to Dr William Sweeney at New York Hospital, who operated on Doris for blocked fallopian tubes. She fell pregnant, then miscarried. Sweeney operated twice more, with no success. He finally suggested an experimental procedure; he would try laparoscopic surgery to withdraw follicular fluid from Doris's ovaries, and this would be mixed with her husband's sperm and incubated by another colleague, Dr Landrum Shettles, who worked nearby at Columbia-Presbyterian Hospital.

This was one of the first IVF experiments in the United States. The Catholic Church had already condemned any fertilisation of eggs outside the human body and in 1969 a poll showed that the majority of Americans believed techniques like IVF were 'against God's will'. Dr Shettles did not clear his in-vitro fertilisation experiments with Columbia-Presbyterian's hospital administration.

On September 12, 1973, John Del Zio took two test tubes containing Doris's follicular fluid on a five-mile cab ride uptown, while Doris recovered from her surgery downtown. Upon arrival, he was directed to a room to masturbate, and Dr Shettles mixed the liquids together. But word of the experiment had reached the administration, and Shettles, along with the test tubes, was summoned to their offices and told that the hospital's federal grants might be compromised by his actions. He was forbidden to continue.

One version of the story has it that the director of Obstetrics and Gynaecology refused to let him leave the room; after a few hours at room temperature, any fertilisation in the test tubes would have failed. Another version is that they removed the corks for good measure. A third version is that this sabotage was quietly done in the lab later on. A fourth is that the test tubes were frozen – and remain, to this day, in a fridge at that hospital.

Doris and John Del Zio weren't informed the experiment had been stopped until hours after the fact. It sent Doris into a deep depression; the month her child would have been born, she woke from a faint in a Florida department store to find her arms full of baby clothes. There is no mention in any of the news reports I could find of what Doris and John's children from their previous marriages thought about any of this. I do not know if Doris and John are still alive, or still in Florida. As the faces of one of the first attempts at in-vitro fertilisation, they flame like comets into history, then out of it.

The Del Zios sued Columbia-Presbyterian Hospital for intentionally inflicting distress and for terminating a procedure that was begun at another institution. (They were eventually awarded $50,000.) A week after the civil suit began, the world's first successful IVF baby, Louise Joy Brown, was born in the United Kingdom, weighing 5 pounds and 12 ounces. Incrementally, step by step, a number of scientists had refined their understanding of the hormones involved in ovulation, of when to withdraw follicular fluid and mix it with sperm, what temperature to incubate it at, and how to transfer the embryo back into the womb. And when it was suddenly possible – when there was a baby girl, smiling, a miracle of flesh and blood on the front page of hundreds of newspapers – public opinion swiftly changed. Clinics began to open at research hospitals across the United States and through the United Kingdom.

It amazes me that IVF is barely older than I am. This is one reason why no history of the rapidly evolving field has been written for the layperson; there is no book that traces the Western discovery of sperm and ova, the identification of hormones involved in ovulation (and how to stimulate this event), or the development of insemination techniques and incubation. It's there, in pieces, in medical journals. There are articles written by psychologists about the grief of infertility. But there is no ethnography of the field, no study of all of the women who were operated on: those anonymous seventeenth-century female corpses, the unnamed patients of Dr Sims and the Doris Del Zios of this world. There is no consideration of the anthropological oddities of this technology and its effects on women, no book about those online message boards (which belong to the Bronze Age of the internet, when the point was not to publicise one's life so much as to explore and participate in communities otherwise out of reach). The chatroom entries feel like old telegraph messages, archaically instrumental. They broadcast basic information, opaque and often puzzling abbreviations, numbers and measurements, emotions in stark, primary colours, emojis for when matters get really complicated. The code that has developed is a counterpoint to Western medicalese. It is a dialect that women you know have quietly and silently learned how to speak. And beyond these message boards, no one really acknowledges it. There is no book that tries to stitch together women's stories, that notes the strange tonal shifts in their conversations with each other, how they – we – swing between the coy and the scientifically explicit, between joy and despair. *This is how I'm going to tell it.*

On the 24th of July, I got my period again. On the 25th, I went in for another round of blood tests. Doctor No. 2's office was in a far swankier building further uptown, but his waiting room was similarly crammed with upholstered chairs in apricot and blue. On each chair sat a numb-looking woman. We did not talk to each other.

When I came out of yoga that afternoon, there was a message on my phone. Another nurse. 'Your FSH is 9. You are going to start treatment tonight.'

And just like that, I could begin. It was Louise Brown's thirty-seventh birthday that day.

For those wondering how and why: I do not know. The doctors do not seem to know why FSH fluctuates either. Large

parts of this process are still a mystery. I rested, I did acupuncture, I drank that Chinese tea.

On the message boards, the 2WW – two-week wait – is the
period of time between ovulation and your next period, which
is the time you have to wait in order to find out if you're
pregnant; if sex, or an IUI (insemination by catheter), or an
embryo transferal (the result of IVF) has actually worked.

But there are other kinds of two-week waits. There is, for
instance, the two weeks of 'stimming'. It was hard to inject
myself that first evening. In order to overcome my evolutionary instinct not to insert a sharp pointed metal object into
myself, I had to talk out loud, to literally tell myself to push
the plunger down.

It grew easier as the days passed. I didn't put on too much
weight. I was very tired one day, and had to leave work early.
I walked incessantly, probably six miles a day. I dreamed of
children. The more swollen my ovaries became, the more I felt
full all the time, as if I had just eaten a large meal. Compared
to other stories on the internet, I had it easy.

The clinic monitors your growing eggs by inserting a slender
rod with a condom on it inside of you. It's called a trans-vaginal
ultrasound. As the days passed, I grew used to the sight of my
follicles – black dots that reminded me of the seeds in dragon
fruit, and later, droplets of balsamic vinegar – swimming into
view, increasing in size as the doctor pushed his way to the left
and the right, measuring their size, calling out numbers to his
aide. I was responding well to the hormones, they said – so well
that I started a third injection each day which slowed down the
follicles' growth a little, allowed them to grow a little more
consistently as a group, rather than the body selecting a 'lead'
follicle (as it normally would). I needed only seven days of the

drugs before they told me I was ready to take my hCG trigger shot. Of course, this worried me; by then, all news was bad news, even if they assured me otherwise.

It was now early August. On the day of retrieval, I sat in a waiting room with six other women, all dressed in hospital gowns, their partners sitting next to them. One by one, they each disappeared into surgery. I was at the Columbia-Presbyterian Medical Center, the same hospital that Doris Del Zio sued. It's since become one of the leading IVF research clinics in the United States. I did the math. The IVF clinic closes for two months a year, but for the rest of the year they see patients seven days a week. In the last year alone, they must have conducted 1800 egg retrievals.

Now it was my turn to walk into the operating room, and climb up onto the table. 'The IV might burn a little,' the anaesthesiologist said. 'It's going in now.'

'Put your left leg up onto the stirrup,' the nurse said, wrapping Velcro straps around it. I don't even remember lifting my right leg.

While I was unconscious, they inserted a catheter-like tube through my vagina, made a small incision into each of my ovaries, and sucked everything out. When I read about the oper-ation beforehand, I couldn't shake the description I'd once read in a cheap horror novel of a shark's stomach contents: a licence plate, fishing twine, a bit of a boot, fish, and parts of a man's torso. They were removing my flotsam.

Two months earlier, when I had made my first appointment with my first doctor, I hadn't even been sure I was there for IVF. I was thinking about simply freezing my eggs, putting them on ice for a relationship and a better point in my career. But my FSH and AMH numbers indicated that my eggs might be poor quality. I would probably be more successful if I froze embryos rather than eggs. Two ex-boyfriends said that they would donate sperm. It was a foolhardy offer, made recklessly, and with love. And I agreed. For all my ambivalence, which has lasted for years, it took one day to decide that there was no need to be unsure anymore.

When I woke up from my retrieval, it was to one of these ex-boyfriends, smiling down at me. He was there to take me home. We went to lunch at a diner nearby; he was starving too, having not eaten in solidarity. We thought of our body parts five blocks away, disembodied, swimming around each other like planets. We prayed for collapses in gravity, and ate tuna melts in silence at the counter, watching the line cook work.

On YouTube, you can watch millions of sperm swarming an egg, covering its surface with their tiny wriggling tails. You can watch ICSI (intracytoplasmic sperm injection) which is when a glass pipette is pushed into an egg (which bends, bends, and then suddenly breaks), and a single sperm makes its way down through the glass tube into the egg, a passenger flight of one.

They retrieved seven eggs. Six were mature. Using ICSI, they were able to successfully fertilise five. I got the call at work, and whooped out loud in the conference room. It was the first bit of great news. I called my ex. 'I'm just so proud,' he said, a little tearful, 'that our bodies could do this.' We just about burst with happiness.

The embryos began to divide: one cell, then two, then four. By day three, ten. We had expected to transfer then, but the embryos were doing so well they decided to grow them out to day five, when an embryo has approximately one hundred cells and is known as a blastocyst. The chance for a successful transfer becomes a lot higher.

Before June, if you had asked me about the image that came to mind when I thought of childbirth, I would have told you that it was the way the aliens hatch through human chest walls in the *Alien* movies: a pulsing, a thrumming below the skin, then *pow*, a small, bloody, penile battering ram punching up and out into the air, mewling like a psychopathic kitten. I assumed I would only see the science of IVF in a similarly alienated way; groups of women in scrubs silently waiting to be harvested, the only penetration by metal and plastic.

But the experience wasn't like that at all. The science, for all its numbers and percentages and studies, felt just as magical as the stories I read as a child. There is a story by Hans Christian Andersen called 'Thumbelina', which begins: 'There was once a woman who wished very much to have a child, but she could not obtain her wish.' I had never thought I would be that woman. She went to a fairy and asked for a child. 'Oh, that can be easily managed,' the fairy said, and gives her a barley-corn 'of a different kind to those which grow in the farmer's fields'. The fairy's matter-of-fact tone reminds me of my second doctor's. *That can be easily managed.* While our embryos were growing in the lab, I lay awake at night and imagined them, six miles away. There was magic in those incubators. Galaxies of human life were expanding and contracting, and in among them were my – our – five planets. It felt a miracle, like a story about a man whose foot was chopped off, and the foot continued to hop about, and then away. My body had life beyond me.

On the fifth day, I visited the hospital again. There were six women again in the waiting room, all dressed in scrubs. The operating room had opera playing. Lab clinicians walked from incubator to lab bench and microscope with one hand cupping the petri dish, the other resting protectively over it. They gave me a photograph of the two embryos they were going to put in, and I felt a fierce pride. 'They're good looking,' the embryologist said.

On YouTube too, you can now watch an ovulation as it happens inside the body; the film was taken by accident during another laparoscopic surgical procedure. It's bloody and mystifying; you see juddering red flesh, even torn-looking, pulsing with the heartbeat, and the emergence of a white drop of liquid that moves, jerking, toward another jagged piece of flesh. There is no obvious sac, no clean tube, no neat baton pass. This looks more like two people bumping into each other in a crowd in slow motion. If you had shown me this video without the title, I never would have guessed what was going on. Our bodies have no interest in our aesthetics. The uterus, contrary to anatomical illustrations, is not actually a hollow-looking vase of flesh. It is a piece of flesh approximately 3 centimetres in length, its walls pressing against each other. After transfer, the embryo does not float around in space like an astronaut, desperately trying to land. Of course, that didn't stop me from worrying. I walked out of the hospital gingerly. I was in a panic to get home and lie down. I began talking to my uterus and to my little blasto-cysts, urging them to burrow into my uterine tissue. I put their photo on my mantelpiece.

That was almost two weeks ago. It is now mid-August, and I am sitting in a white wooden chair on a hill in Maine, on holiday with the other ex. For the past two days, I have watched hummingbirds hover less than a foot away, drinking from the sugar-water feeder hanging from the deck. The hum of their wings is loud enough for me to always stop what I am writing, and watch. Their bodies are stout with summer.

I have spent this summer waiting; waiting to start, then waiting to end, then waiting to transfer, and now waiting for implantation. Nothing may have changed. Everything may have.

In the two-week wait, it is tempting to avoid social occasions where people will ask how you are. You cannot drink. You are unusually risk-averse. As if you were ill, you are strangely deliberate about what to do with your energy. Do you dare jumping into that waterhole? What about staying in the sun all day, dehydrated and hungry? The hope that you are pregnant slowly begins to build, like algal bloom in a pond. You inspect your breasts. Are they bigger? Every stomach twinge is interpreted as implantation cramps. You never thought of yourself as a nauseated person, but now you feel butterflies all of the time. You find yourself smiling. It's hard to organise holidays or plane flights. You are constantly delaying decisions. Nonetheless, you try to avoid calculating your due date and fail.

On the seven-hour drive north, we listened to an audio-book version of Marcel Proust's *In Search of Lost Time*. I picked it because that phrase has repeatedly come to mind when I think about the last few months. Marcel is a sickly boy, in love with the women in his life, terrified by the men. The adults around him are his world, but he can't understand their indifference to him and each other. And they can't understand what is important to him: the terror of the night, a kiss before bedtime, a cry from the garden, a biscuit dipped in tea. I looked out of the car window at the endless line of trees bursting with life, and thought of my own childhood, how remote it seemed. I marvelled at all the things I wouldn't understand about my own child, and how this didn't matter at all, because the love I already felt had charged the rest of my world with meaning.

In the last few days, we have visited stores that sell fudge and tiny quartz bears. We've watched children swim in the lake, and read and dreamed through the afternoons that seem to stretch on forever. I have thought about the summers I would like to give a child, but only in broad, vague shapes, like the blue hills in the distance; it is still too painful to think about in any detail. Yet I am no longer entirely averting my gaze. I have thought a lot about the women whose stories I have read these past few months, who were willing for their loss to be counted. I owe them.

Online, there are many articles about the two-week wait, about how to bear the seemingly endless stretch of days (television, treating yourself, new cooking techniques, tackling small jobs), but they all seem to miss what makes the two-week wait particularly unbearable, which is the fact that women suffering fertility issues go through this two-week wait over and over again. At the end of two weeks, you might find out that you weren't really waiting; you are not pregnant, and you were not really living your life the way you wanted to, and now those two weeks are gone and it's time to start all over again. You are always waiting, preparing, postponing your life for another that may never come.

Those first few days after transfer, the knowledge that two living creatures were inside me was strong; it coloured everything like a kind of light filter. Now, it has become a binary. They are dead, or alive. And even if they are alive, they might be chromosomally abnormal; statistically speaking, 50 per cent of a 35-year-old woman's eggs are abnormal.

I have practised yoga almost every day for years now, and thought I knew my body fairly well. This is because I had grown proficient at isolating my awareness to particular parts. I understand, for example, how the ribs on my right side are working in relation to the inward rotation of the left thigh in a pose. But this does not help me now. I do not know what is going on inside of me. I had always thought the mind/body distinction pretty spurious – there are so many forms of knowledge that grow from the body, that are embroidered upon by the mind (and vice versa) – but I have started to feel otherwise. My body has cut me off, is not speaking to me yet. I feel utterly normal, and I am afraid of what this means.

Two times in the past four days, we've visited the local hospital for blood tests to check my hormone levels. If I'm not pregnant, these results might give them a clue as to why it didn't work. Tomorrow, we visit for one last test: a blood pregnancy test. The two-week wait will be up.

Before June, time sluiced through me like a waterfall. Now, I feel more like an old-fashioned watermill. The minutes fill me up, like drops of water in a cup at the end of each paddle. Time moves so slowly, but it adds up – till I brim, brim, then over I go again, with a splash.

Tina Makereti
This Compulsion in Us

The year is 1979. I'm five years old, walking into the Wanganui
Museum, hand in hand with my father. I wear woollen
tights and buckled shoes and most days there doesn't seem
to be much difference between what I can see and what I can
imagine. On my fifth birthday I had been so disappointed by
my playdough kindergarten birthday cake, I had tried to eat
it, having decided the act of believing would magically transform it into something sweetly edible. Already, real life has
proven itself fraught, though I have found solace in story-
books. At home I spend hours drawing cinderella dresses over
and over – tightly cinched waists, crinolines, pannier skirts.
In Wanganui Museum, approaching the Edwardian Street,
I travel back in time: olden day shops with toys and sweets, a
living room, mannequins with real cinderella dresses. I have
no concept of the era, only that this is as close to the imagi-
nary world of story as I am likely to get.

And there is Dad's hand: dry and warm, large and solid and
square-fingered. When he lets go to point out objects from his
own childhood, there is his voice, telling stories about how
things were done in the old days, how it was different, more
pure and innocent it seems, even to a five-year-old. Later we
climb the stairs and view the animals and birds that have

First published in *Landfall* 229, May 2015.

  In this essay, 'Wanganui' refers to the town of my childhood, while 'Whanganui'
refers to the contemporary place. 'Whanganui' is the correct spelling, but the
original colonial spelling, and all it represents, seems more apt here.

stitches showing, glass eyes and stuffing that springs out at alarming angles. Somehow this is all part of the crusty magic of the place.

In 1991 I return with my first year Museum Studies class. I am excited about going back to the first museum I can remember – we haven't lived in Wanganui since I was six. But I walk in with the newly acquired weight of family and cultural history bearing down on my shoulders. I reach the first cabinet in the Māori Court – a glass box filled with count-less taonga pounamu – and stop. I feel inexplicably bad. Dizzy, almost as if I have stepped outside of myself. I have learnt enough in my Māori art and culture papers to know that these hei pounamu, hei tiki and hei matau once adorned the physical bodies of ancestors, and had likely been separated from those tūpuna by warfare, poverty or sneaky dealings. I know that the creation of taonga pounamu was a long, laborious process that took generations to complete. I know that the taonga most likely still carry the mana and tapu of their original makers and wearers, and the number of items lined up row upon row tells me that they were acquired care-lessly, without reverence for their intrinsic value as anything other than exotic objects.

I turn and leave. On my way out I try to express my dismay to a fellow Māori student, but he does not seem to feel as bad as I do. I wonder now whether it was the swiftness of two inner worlds coming together that caused my out of body discord. As a child I had not found the Māori Court interesting. I don't remember taking more than a cursory glance at the items there. Back then, Māori culture was taken for granted by mainstream New Zealand, and I had not learnt to see its value. I certainly had not learnt the stories behind any taonga I saw, and a trip to the museum wouldn't have taught me them.

This is no longer the case, of course. When I visit what is now called the Whanganui Regional Museum in 2013 I meet staff working with both the history of the objects and the ironies of the history of their institution. These days, there is a level of self-awareness evident in most museums that was beginning to flourish around the time I went there as a first-year student. You wouldn't find a bulk cabinet of pounamu on display today, but you would find curators and conservators and registrars in basements and backrooms, trying to bring the disparate pieces of history back together, making connections between objects and people, looking for the source of things.

Kanohi ki te Kanohi

When I arrive at the Museum der Weltkulturen in 2012, there is an exhibition installed on the ground floor of Villa 37. On the third floor are the apartments a small group of New Zealand artists and writers will share for the next month. Villa 37, Schaumainkai, overlooks the Main River, Frankfurt, along what is known as Museumsufer or the Museum Embankment, named for the large concentration of museums in that area. The city is old and pretty. The locals are friendly and multi-lingual and uber-elegant. Even the children and dogs appear languid.

The exhibition is called *Face to Face*, or *Fa'afesaga'i* in Sāmoan, *Kanohi ki te Kanohi* in Māori. It contains pen and ink drawings by young Sāmoan-Kiwi artist Francis Pesamino alongside taonga from the Weltkulturen Polynesian collection. I haven't seen contemporary Polynesian drawings by an emerging artist exhibited alongside tatau instruments and carved taonga before. The mix of ancient and modern is illuminating, creating associations a New Zealander, with all our education and cultural awareness, might not make. How does a portrait of Valerie Adams, her sponsor's name like a tattoo on her collar, resonate with ancient tatau patterns and carvings, for example? How does who we were in the past relate to who we are now?

The resonances of *Face to Face / Kanohi ki te Kanohi / Fa'afesaga'i* increase as the days go by. At a press conference Tanea Heke, who is director of the New Zealand at Frankfurt programme, speaks of this concept – the relationships we have formed and how we have all come to be in this space at this time. We all bring, she tells the German media, our people with us.

The exhibition opens, and there is a bit of celebratory mingling. At this event Yvette Mutumba, the curator of the African collection, asks about my visits to Weltkulturen's other collections. I tell her my main observation, which is how much everyone loves and cares for their collections. She tells me that in Germany they do not use the word 'curator' for their work, but 'Kustodin'. This word gives a clearer picture of what their work is, she says, opening her arms wide like a bird taking chicks under its wings – they look after the objects. I immediately think of how close the idea of custodianship is to kaitiakitanga. It is not the first time I have found myself thinking that the way they do things here is closer to the way we do things at home than I thought they would be.

The collections of the Weltkulturen are vast, and this is unsettling. The institution's main benefactors were collectors in the days when the objective was to obtain as many different examples of one type of thing as possible, in order to swap items with other institutions. Before I left New Zealand, I asked a curator friend if there was anything I should do to prepare for an encounter with taonga that had been taken overseas. She told me that when she was in Berlin she had been taken without warning into a room filled with shelves of skulls. Better to write ahead and tell them I didn't want to see any human remains, she advised. And whakanoa (cleanse with water) whenever possible. The Kustodins are very mindful of my request, though the director, Clémentine Deliss, tells me about the mokomokai that have been repatriated to Te Papa, and assumes I will want to see images of them.

Our 'job' as writers and artists in residence is to respond to the collections at the museum. A fresh eye on things can bring new ways of relating to and interpreting collections. This method was instituted only recently as a way to approach an old museum problem that had been exacerbated by World War II: all the taonga had been saved because they had been sent out of the city; all the museum records had not. While colonial collection records may have been inadequate, they would have been better than none at all.

The medieval city of Frankfurt was flattened by the war. Afterwards, it was impossible to recreate the worn beauty of stone edifices imbued with history. Clémentine tells me how even now the city plans historical recreations into their rebuilds, striving for some sort of pre-World War II authenticity that no longer exists. The town centre, Römerberg, is disdainfully referred to as Disneyland by locals. Postcards for sale all around Römerberg display Frankfurt at different stages of annihilation, pre-annihilation, and reconstruction. The famous Römer is a facsimile of something Frankfurt lost to successive bombs that ended 5500 lives.

Soon Clémentine is herding us towards a table of food, like a very European marae auntie. 'Eat, eat! Come and sit down! You must eat. Where's Francis?' As the youngest in our crew, and the freshest to overseas travel, Francis is the subject of much concern, which gives us ample opportunity to tease him – 'You've got some German aunties now, eh? Bet you weren't expecting that.'

Later, I think about how perfect the title of the exhibition is as a symbol for what is happening at the museum. *Kanohi ki te kanohi* is an oft-repeated Māori proverb that suggests that communication is better served by face-to-face meetings. Traditionally, Māori implicitly trust face-to-face contact as a means of avoiding misunderstandings and misinterpretations. The effort undertaken to meet face to face also suggests a level of respect and keenness to establish effective relationships. It's like shaking hands or sharing food – a communal, physical gesture of relationality. Or the pōwhiri ritual of encounter, which forces visitors and hosts to lay bare their intentions, antagonisms and interconnections. I imagine that someone from the New Zealand at Frankfurt team must have suggested this title, but when I ask Dr Eva Raabe, who curated the exhibition, I find this is not the case.

Eva's idea was that Francis' portraits and the objects from the collection would face each other, and that viewers would face them. Clémentine suggested the name Face to Face, and Eva agreed. Only then were translations into Māori and Sāmoan made. Because I don't believe in coincidences of this scale, I like to think that the staff involved in putting together the exhibition had developed some sensitivity to the cultural resonances of the objects with which they work. How else could a concept so fundamental to Māori culture have found its way into their lexicon as they worked with objects from Aotearoa? Māori believe that our taonga are living, breathing representations of the ancestors – could this not be one way they show that indeed they are already in dynamic relationship, kanohi ki te kanohi, with their guardians in this institution?

'Taonga are our time-travellers,' says Paul Tapsell in his 2011 Gordon H. Brown Lecture. 'They made real not only the ancestors, but also their surrounding landscapes by burying a sense of ancestral belonging deep into our living core.' Taonga, he explains, collapse time so that descendants can emotionally engage and experience ancestral moments in the now. Perhaps even non-descendants can pick up echoes of meaning from these emissaries of time and place.

Later, during one of the collection visits, Eva admits to one of the Kiwi visitors that at times of stress or conflict she touches the objects and talks to them. This information is eagerly passed among us. Later, when I ask her about it, she speaks of the very oldest stone objects, barely identifiable, which seem to carry a deep feeling of strength and calm. Perhaps her colleagues would disparage her for such actions, she says, but she has risen in our already high esteem.

If I had any preconceptions, it was that I had expected to perceive the containment of Māori taonga in institutions like Weltkulturen in terms of our loss, but instead I discover a sense of exchange and yearning. The older impetus to collect objects, to colonise and contain, I do not understand. But now that the collections are there, custodians and audiences display a curiosity that is more unguarded and receptive than snatching and appropriative. The objects in the collection hold a charge that, as much as possible, is honoured, rather than suppressed. This is not without its risks, but the practice recognises that museum collections contain taonga – precious objects that allow us to touch something ancient and deep and much more knowing than we are.

Before we leave, we are to take part in discussions and readings as part of the Frankfurt Book Fair. One quiet afternoon, I take the key we have been given and go downstairs to sit with the taonga and write. On the day I am to leave, I take an audience into the same room, and ask them to face the canoe prow, or tauihu, displayed there. I tell them the story the taonga tells me, of history, wars and appropriations, losses and connections; of time passing and two nations brought together, face to face.

In Case You See Yourself

Passing through the main entrance of the Canterbury Museum, visitors are confronted by life-sized dioramas of Māori from the moa hunter period. They are posed in classical style: a stuffed moa in the foreground, a man with a spear crouched near him, ready to throw; a woman squatted low with her kurī at her side, their faces drawn in anticipation. In a sense, it is a beautifully rendered scene. Elsewhere, a woman leans over her waka, fish in one hand, breasts drooping realistically over her canoe. Men engage various technologies, making fire and flint, houses and storehouses in the background; a woman cooks small birds on a kind of spit. The scenes are as real as any that can be viewed in the best museum dioramas in the world, the human forms and expressions carefully moulded. I've seen worse recreations of colonial European figures: loose beards and frightening eyes, arms drooping where elbows and muscle-tone should be. They've done a good job: so much detail and depth.

Faces and voices from all over the world move swiftly past these entrance-way dioramas. When they stop, it is for no more than thirty seconds or so. One or two walk slowly, peer more carefully, but none stay as I do. What do they see? I wonder. How do they read these displays? And then, do they see me? I begin to feel as if I am a later manifestation of the people in the cases. Few would think that. Few would look at the half-naked, brown-skinned, dark-haired figures in the cases and make a connection with the light-skinned, red-haired, clothed figure beside them. But if they look more closely, they might see the broad nose, thick lips and fuzzy hair. Perhaps even that would not be enough, but what would they conclude if I looked more like my ancestors? What if I looked like my cousins?

A pre-teen girl comes through the gallery, gawping at my still-life friend with her fish and her waka, bare-breasted and bent forwards for all eternity, and exclaims loudly, 'Soooo not appropriate!' like a character from *Mean Girls*. I almost laugh aloud. She's right, of course, in more ways than she's aware of.

The dioramas are a window to a version of the past: 3D fabricated stills of history or 'pre-history' that happen to fit a particular way of viewing the world, evolution, history and technology. Move to the next room and quite a different picture emerges. Here objects *made* by people in centuries past can be viewed – adzes, carved pou, ancestral figures, fish hooks. In this room, I overhear a mother say to her son, 'Look how they were able to turn that piece of rock into a tool.' Here there is the opportunity to understand how the ancestors lived via the material goods they left behind. Imaginations have to be engaged. Viewers slow down and are forced to engage with the display more carefully.

Furthermore, the objects are imbued with their own power. That power might simply be a kind of archaeological and historical patina, or it may be the inherent power left by the makers of the objects, otherwise known as mana and tapu. To some, these museum artefacts carry the stories of everything that has happened to them and their people. A kind of nexus is therefore possible between the museum visitor, the object, and the people who long ago created and used it. A quiet walk around the gallery might create in the viewer a sense of awe. In this, there is a kind of magic.

The artefacts are presented in a way that suggests they signify a progression from the moa hunter dioramas. But if the hypothesis, based primarily on Eurocentric analysis of material goods, is that as time went on, Māori developed a more cultivation-based, stratified and 'sophisticated' culture, then something is wrong. The people represented by the dioramas didn't spring from the ground fully formed, nor did they evolve from apes in a land that knew no mammals. They navigated their way here following star maps and sea paths their ancestors had devised over centuries of experience and careful observation. The arrival of wave after wave of mighty sea-voyaging waka was not accidental, nor were their return voyages or other explorations. They brought with them the animals and plants they needed to survive, sent their strongest and cleverest men and women, including tohunga and ran-gatira. These were people who knew the constellations, winds, currents and their own technologies so well they could con-fidently sail for months to settle an uninhabited land. They represented a level of knowledge and sophistication that few of us could claim. The dioramas, carefully rendered though they might be, show none of this.

In contrast, most contemporary museums[*] are moving towards interactive, story-based exhibitions that contextualise historical experiences. Which is essential, since representing human figures without voice to express their stories continues a line of thinking that takes us, if we follow it to its natural con-clusion, to dark and inhumane territory.

[*] Including Canterbury, I suspect.

Looking at the diorama figures, I can't help wondering how far they are from other aspects of the natural history collection. All other living things were collected and stuffed by naturalists in vast quantities to be shared with other museums all over the world. Brian Gill's *The Owl that Fell from the Sky: Stories of a Museum Curator* explains the world of taxidermy and categorisation, collection and taxonomy. Gill is passionate about the need for such collection and preservation. 'Fully documented natural history specimens are called "voucher specimens"', he writes. 'Each provides a documentary record of biological occurrence and distribution that is superior to a mere literature record . . . As natural history collections grow they become massive directories of the animals and plants that have lived in different areas at different times, and may hold the key to how the characteristics and distributions of species have varied with place and changed with time.' Gill goes on to give many examples of how natural history collections have been useful for conservation and scientific discovery. More important for research than the mounted specimens we can view in museums are 'study-skins. These require the same skilled taxidermy but for easy storage and examination they are set out straight, like a human body laid in a coffin.' Sets of loose bones are also essential for identification work, as are the 'bones of an individual joined together as an articulated skeleton', and animals preserved in alcohol.

What I make of this is not Brian Gill's fault. Even as I nod along with his naturalist's enthusiasm, uncertainty marks my reading. I waver between two extremes. I have enjoyed museums and their collections all my life. I have come close to (admittedly dead) animals I never would have seen, and learnt much from the experience, but something about this is inherently uncomfortable. It is not a far leap to wonder, while viewing Canterbury Museum's moa hunter dioramas, whether museums would have taxidermied humans if it had been ethically possible.

This might seem an extreme position until one considers that naturalists did once collect human bones, especially skulls, to categorise different ethnic groups and genders according to cranial size; that living humans were displayed in museums and zoos until at least a third of the way into the twentieth century; that in the Canterbury Museum itself, a fully intact Egyptian mummy is displayed, her wrappings intact but her body x-rayed, researched and scanned for all that she can reveal about her people; that in our national museum, Te Papa, human remains were an element of the recent Aztec exhibition. If there were some acceptable way to preserve the human form posed in action, just like the birds and mammals of the Antarctic exhibition, wouldn't they have done it? What if there were Neanderthal remains that could be resurrected to look natural? Would that be more acceptable, like stuffed mammoths or orangutans? Imagine the benefits to science and the potential audience. How human is too human?

How naïve of me to ask. A little more research reveals study-skins and bones of humans were collected. I've known for some time about Khoikhoi woman Sara Baartman, who was exhibited in Britain and Europe while alive, and whose bones and body cast were exhibited in France for decades after her death, until she was finally repatriated to South Africa and given the dignity of proper burial. I am unprepared for where a little more research takes me (look away, sensitive readers): 'In the nineteenth century . . . many Khoikhoi women were treated as taxidermic material, their skins stripped and stuffed to preserve them as specimens of the anomalous. Sir John Herschel, during his visit to the Cape in the mid-1830s, noted that he had seen a "Hottentot woman's skin – stuffed . . . with all the extraordinary peculiarities attributed to these nymphs by travellers".[*]

So we are not so far from our animal cousins. Some of us more than others, apparently.

The Museum in the Living Room

Here is the paradox of the museum: it preserves and contains treasures, but also captures and immobilises things which make sense only in motion, things that should breathe and transform. The uncontainable. The living. Somewhere in the centre of that paradox is the niggling discomfort that accompanies each visit. In Frankfurt, even though we lived on the top floor of a museum building, it was on visiting a friend that I encountered a place that was like a museum without the more worrying aspects of museology. Barbara is a film-maker who had come to Aotearoa to make a documentary about New Zealand writers, and then invited two of her subjects for dinner during our time in her home city. We followed her around the aromatic and colourful Kleinmarkthalle, where fresh and hand-crafted deli foods of all kinds could be bought. Then she took us to her small apartment on a narrow street that I remember as cobbled (Barbara assures me that it is not). In a walled garden we ate and drank and talked, then went inside where she fed us delicate pasta parcels with the ubiquitous, sharp rucola salad. We talked about books and film-making and stopped open-mouthed when Barbara told

---

[*] 'Collecting Bodies: Some perspectives on Sarah Baartman', Collecting New Media, 13 February 2013: blogs.ischool.utexas.edu/newmedia/2012/02/13/collecting-bodies-some-perspectives-on-sarah-baartman

us stories about her other film projects – the time she filmed 'Marty' (Scorsese) talking to film students, her decision to concentrate her documentary skills on the quieter arts like writing.

Barbara's place was tiny and warren-like, shelves filled wall space with records and books to the ceiling. The upper floors included her office space, kitchen, and living areas, but where we entered, on the bottom floor, was full of older wooden furniture, and paintings. When I asked her permission to write about this, she sent me a document with photos of the building just after World War II, when it was a bakery. I recognised the outer walls of the garden courtyard we had sat in. In 1976 she moved in, her father taking the downstairs in 1980 as his studio. Almost forty years later, she hopes to go on renting her home despite rapidly rising rents.

Barbara's father would have turned a hundred last year, so she staged an exhibition of his work at Frankfurt's oldest half-timber house, which dates from the twelfth century. As she notes, Georg Dickenberger was a brilliant man, his paintings vivid and soulful, sometimes abstract. 'As they were rather poor he did not have extensive schooling, but he acquired an enormous knowledge by reading. He was my Google and Wikipedia long before the internet – about history or art you could ask him anything.' After they died, she restored all her parents' nice old (and half broken) furniture and took it with their books over to the studio. 'And now it feels like home.'

More than a museum, then. We were only there one evening, but I think of it as often as the Weltkulturen. We had been welcomed and fed and shown a piece of the history of a city, kept alive and warm by a descendant, and her stories.

Going to the Zoo

For six months in 2014, we are residents at Randell Cottage, Thorndon, built in 1867. Randell Cottage also has a museum in the living room – on our second day I discover the purpose of the small cabinet beside the bookshelf. It houses items that were excavated from under and within the house during renovation: nineteenth-century bottles and toys and crockery. The house is a mix of the original and the reconstructed or re-envisioned. Despite the care given to the reconstructed, it is the original elements that hold an extra charge: floorboards made from ship's timbers, original brick around a fireplace, glass windows over walls that show layers of original wallpaper. Outside there is a plaque under the ngaio tree, and another on the gate. We live in a house with signage denoting its age and cultural value.

My project for the residency is to write a novel based on the story of a boy who was taken to London to be exhibited alongside George French Angas's drawings and paintings in the mid-nineteenth century. Very little is known about the real boy and his life. The first book I pick up inside the cottage is *The Fox Boy* by Peter Walker, which is about a different 'orphaned' Māori boy in the nineteenth century. I have always wanted to read it, though it seems perfectly apt that I never have until this moment. The abduction of children of one culture by people of another culture traverses a gap, says Walker, and is 'part of a very old theme, of removal and transformation . . . This is worth examining for a moment. The child wanders into the gap, but the gap is not a real place, it exists only in the mind. In other words it is not so much that the child is in the gap, as that the gap is in the child.' The project of transplanting a child fulfils some need within the coloniser to understand the other, but only to such an extent that the gap can be filled with the colonising culture.

Imaginatively, writing this story will take me to Piccadilly Circus, where Indigenous peoples were exhibited along-side exotic animals, material culture, 'freaks' and curiosities. It may also take me back to Frankfurt, where two years ago, on one of our research forays into the Weltkulturen's vast photography, film and document archive, I discovered a folder filled with posters advertising the exhibition of human groups at the Zoologischen Garten. From around 1878 to 1931, in a circus tent on zoo grounds, European audiences were invited to observe such phenomena as the 1885 Ceylon Expedition, featuring 51 Singhalesen and 12 Elephanten; the Ofrikaner-Karawane exhibition, featuring 16 men, 4 women and 7 children; Das Amazonencorps; Australian Cannibal Boomerang Throwers; Krao The Missing Link Half Monkey Half Woman; and Schaustellung der Samoaner-Truppe (Flaunt the Sāmoan Troup, according to Google).

Later exhibition posters for Sāmoan groups are somewhat in keeping with one Weltkulturen Kustodin's comment that Sāmoan groups were treated better than the African or Asian groups that came. 'Our new compatriots' crows one poster above the title 'Ausstellung Samoa'. The S for Sāmoa is formed by a snake wrapped around the top half of a seductive, heavy-lidded temptress dressed only in a tooth necklace with a flower tucked above one ear.

The truth is, I am compelled by these posters not only for the historical story they tell, but for the exotic whiff they exude. They are odd, and old, romanticised and beautiful. Whatever horrifying tale they tell, I am just as voyeuristic about it as the audiences that would have flocked to the zoo for entertainment. Would that I could watch those audiences as they watched the people forced to parade or perform for their pleasure. How did we reach the moment in history that made such an activity acceptable? Desirable? Shouldn't I be more repelled by this story? I am strangely attracted to it, understanding the dehumanisation in intellectual terms, but unable to instinctually reject a story that tells me something about what human beings are, what we are capable of.*

The old and odd. I want to understand this compulsion in us. The freak show. The talk show. Reality TV. The world's biggest, or smallest, or grossest, or oldest. A moment on the internet is enough to show we haven't moved far from putting people in zoos, and making assumptions, and feeling superior. The modern museum may have an uncomfortable relationship with this, removing itself through changes in focus and display and interpretation. And so it should. But inside me is still the child who was fascinated by the old and dusty exhibits in Wanganui – the (forgive me) *weirdness* of it all, and it's she who sometimes drives the writing.

And maybe it's she who turns me to history as a place of refuge and solace, as a place I can pick apart and puzzle back together, as a place that despite all its tragedies and travesties, is infinitely more comfortable to spend time with than the harsh realities and uncertainties of the heaving, polluted, terrifying world as it is now. She seeks comfort, and the museum is like a book: full of adventure, mystery, the vastness of time and travel, all contained and manageable and seemingly safe. Sometimes the museum is where we encounter the 'other', and if we look closely enough, understand that we are looking at some fantastic version of ourselves.

---

* On the other hand, my investigation of taxidermy took me to a place I'd rather not have had to witness.

Going Home

Why is Wanganui Museum the one I remember best, of them all? Why, after living in at least eight places between the ages of three and thirteen, do I think of the town I lived in for barely two years as closest to my home town? Looking back from over here, from this different place, this different time, I see the footsteps my family left all over town. My grand-parents took up residence there in the mid-twentieth century and didn't leave until they took leave of their terrestrial lives. There was the bike shop, the schools, the yearly routines. My father, aunts and uncles grew up there. With their families they made homes and careers, and left, and came back. I barely knew most of them, but perhaps that is all it takes for a place to become a cornerstone in a life. I see now the ghosts of significant places and events: first school, first best friend, first memories, not-quite-first trauma. Whanganui has a res-onance that other places we lived never carried. They don't carry the same draw, the same vibration as a town that bears a familial stamp.

Sometimes, the museum is where we go to find parts of ourselves we thought we'd left behind. On the day we return to Whanganui so I can research this essay, we also visit my father, who has found his way back to one of his home towns. I haven't seen him for nearly three years. As we pull into the driveway I glimpse him in the kitchen, the still-solid hand unsteady now, square finger and thumb pinched around his cigarette as he inhales. He turns and at first I am not sure he has registered our presence because he doesn't move toward us, and his expression does not change. I can already see this will not be a good day. I steel myself to leave the van. As we approach the house, my father comes out and blocks our way. I try to draw him in, promising a lunch he shows no interest in. He makes a couple of jokes about our car and how hard it must be to live with me. For the next hour, he reminds me of a scratched 33 LP, being played too slow, the needle jumping back to the same point and repeating the same out-of-tune warble. He doesn't drink, but his half-full glass waits for him in the fridge. My daughter watches warily. My partner laughs politely. I make food.

An hour later, before I have figured out how we can make a graceful exit, my father says, *Well, it was nice to see ya*. He has gained some lucidity, with the food and the talk. But neither of us seem to have the stamina or forbearance for this kind of encounter.

This last memory is not really about a museum. I don't know if it is really about my father either. Last time we talked he was positive, almost wise. *Most people are basically decent, you know*, he said. I hadn't even told him I had been struggling to live with the world I heard about in the news. That world was not of my making, or my choice. That was a world that had begun to look increasingly ugly and threatening. It was a private pain, but fathers know things.

Sometimes we have to excavate the good from things we have always viewed as bad. Appropriations, lost families, colonised and hidden histories, these are all part of our family stories, not just our national ones. There are always things that are hard to take, things for which we seek solace. But this my father gave me: afternoons at the museum.

Megan Dunn

The Ballad of Western Barbie

Two things happen in Huntly: something and nothing. Sometimes it's hard to tell which is which.

At the age of seven I lived in the brick presbytery next to
the brick church and the Catholic school on Main Street.
I watched Olivia Newton-John in *Grease* at the local cinema,
but otherwise Huntly seemed untouched by glamour and I
was not happy to be there. My mother and I had decamped
from Auckland to the presbytery to live with my grandparents,
who kept house for the priest.

Don't worry. It's not one of those stories. The priest was
polite and sweet, like the scones he ate after church. Inside
the presbytery hallway a statue of Mary stood on a polished
wooden table. Mary had cold feet. So did my mother. We were
in Huntly because of Mum's cold feet. She had left Bruce, a
truck driver, and the father of my half-brother. Mum had an
epiphany after the birth of my half-brother. The epiphany
was that she didn't love Bruce and she wasn't sure she loved
my brother either.

Western Barbie accompanied us on our exodus to Huntly.
Barbie brought her palomino, Dallas, along for the ride. We had
left Auckland in a hurry and Western Barbie only had the outfit
she came in: a white jumpsuit with tassels that upon reflection
was quite Liberace. She took her accessories to Huntly too, a
blue autograph stamp and a set of hairbrushes. Western Barbie

First published on 7 July 2014 in *The Pantograph Punch*: pantograph-punch.com had a lever on her back. If I pushed it down, she'd wink. I like to think that because Barbie was a cowgirl she was in a better position to deal with Huntly. We attended Catholic school together as Barbie and I were close friends and she'd never leave a girl in a crisis. Only for a man and a good time.

At the presbytery, Mum and I slept in single beds in an open-plan bedroom next door to my grandparents. In the evenings, Western Barbie took long baths in her doll-sized turquoise tub and flushed her pink doll-sized loo. Dallas grazed on a patch of wild floral carpet. Barbie had loved and left a man too. When we lived with Bruce, Barbie had been seeing Action Man. Barbie and Action Man had known one another's bodies in the nude, but their plastic arms and legs weren't built right for cuddling. Sex was accompanied by the cold disjointed sound of clacking. Once they rode around Bruce's house in Action Man's tank. Later, they would drink doll-sized glasses of wine. Maybe they talked of war, but I doubt it. Action Man, like Bruce, kept to himself.

We were only in Huntly for six months, but I remember that time as having the long drawn-out qualities of a soap opera. Not so much as a tumbleweed ambled along Main Street. Huntly seemed inhabited by the second-hand clothes mannequins in the window of the Salvation Army store. One pub. One cinema: Olivia Newton-John's wholesome smile on the fading poster by the door. At least church every Sunday was a social occasion. I slotted the autograph stamp on to Barbie's hand, just in case she met any of her fans.

'This is the body of Christ.'

I opened my mouth and the priest placed a pale wafer on my tongue.

The body of Christ dissolved.

'What does it taste like?' Barbie asked.

'Nothing,' I said.

'Shhh.' Nana put her finger to her lips.

The priest moved in front of the altar in his lapping white robes. Above his head was a brass Jesus nailed to a cross and above Jesus was a round window. Clouds chugged past.

The priest said, 'Let us give thanks to the Lord our God.'

The congregation answered, 'It is right to give him thanks and praise.'

The collection basket was passed backwards along the pews. People dropped coins into its wicker rim. Inside the basket spare change jingled and rang out like notes from a tambourine. After church, the congregation gathered outside on the steps. Many people stopped and talked to the priest as though he was a pop star. They shook his hand. 'Thank you for the sermon today, Father.'

On Sunday afternoons, Mum took long walks. Barbie saddled up Dallas and we trailed along. We crossed the rusted railway bridge to the other side of town. The trains seemed infrequent, the business they were designed to do long over-taken. 'Whoa!' Barbie pulled on Dallas's reins. We stopped mid-way across the bridge. Mum stared down at the slow-moving Waikato River. The water was silver where the light struck it, like Western Barbie's tassels. But most of the time it was just brown and murky. Barbie and I surveyed the Huntly Power Station; its two red turrets poked up into the sky. The steeple of the church also reached into the sky. But the chimneys of the power station reached higher.

'I don't believe in God,' Western Barbie said, and I had a lot of respect for her point of view. Barbie was made in a factory. The small of her back was embossed with a copy-right logo and the message: 'Mattel Inc.' Barbie had met her maker, and she told me there had been nothing religious about it. 'My head spun round and round in a rotomould. It was dark. Something sucked me out of the darkness. I heard a pop.' She described her journey along the assembly line on a conveyor belt: 'The women wore little blue hats on their heads that looked like shower caps. They slotted my arms and legs to my body. Then they put on my head.' Her two-tone nylon hair was stitched into her scalp by a sewing machine.

'Did it hurt?'

'A little,' Barbie said. 'But it was worth it.'

I swept the hairbrush through her hair then pressed down the lever on her back.

Barbie was made in Taiwan, but her wink was more or less universal. A team of Mattel employees had taken swatches of fabrics for her white jumpsuit and drawn the prototype for her white cowboy hat and matching cowboy boots. Their designs were inspired by the Country and Western revival that swept across America in the late '70s and early '80s: Western Barbie originally came with several photographs (of herself). I assume she was meant to be a famous Nashville singer; the autograph stamp supplied her signature. By the time we arrived in Huntly, Barbie didn't have any photographs left. I can only hope she gave one to Action Man when they said 'so long'.

*

The afternoon sun melted into the river and the Huntly Power Station chugged smoke into the sky. Barbie tugged on Dallas's reins. By the time we reached the presbytery, sandflies studded the light outside the back door. Western Barbie kicked off her cowboy boots and sat on the edge of her doll-sized double bed and put her head in her hands.

'I wonder what you'll think of me when you're older?'

'What do you mean?'

'I wonder if you'll judge me?'

'Don't cry.'

'I just feel so alone'

'But you're not alone, I'm here. And Dallas too.'

*

A burst of white light: in my school photograph I'm buck-toothed and pig-tailed, dressed in a green tartan pinafore. Behind my head, an electric halo, some weird effect from the photographer's flash. I didn't have an autograph stamp, so my portrait remains unsigned.

*

'Forgive me Father, for I have sinned.'

The priest sat on the other side of the grille.

His palms pressed together in prayer; he turned a string of rosary beads between his fingertips.

The pew creaked as I reached for my sins.

'I swore at a boy in school.'

'I didn't help Nana with the dishes.'

'I have thought bad things about my mother.'

The priest told me to say a 'Hail Mary'. He closed the maroon curtain and the grille disappeared from view. The afternoon sun melted into the river and the Huntly Power Station chugged smoke into the sky.

*

Huntly was originally a Māori settlement called Rāhui Pōkeka, but became a military post during the Waikato Land Wars and a Pākehā settlement afterwards. The Scottish post-master in 1870, James Henry, named Huntly after his home town in Aberdeenshire. Henry used to press an old 'Huntley

Lodge' stamp on to the town's mail. The town still wears his autograph.

Long before James Henry stepped off the boat with the stamp from Huntley Lodge in his luggage, the Māori were using local coal or 'waro' for cooking. The population of Huntly expanded after commercial coalmining began around 1876. It's been suggested that coal was one of the reasons that Pākehā invaded the Waikato in 1863. They wanted control of the seams that run throughout the area. At first coal was mined underground on the east side, until the bridge was built across the Waikato River in 1915, providing access to more coal. The bridge now links East Huntly to West Huntly where the power station resides; two chimneys stretching smoke into the sky.

The Huntly Power Station runs on local coal and gas and uses water from the Waikato River for cooling. Each of its red chimneys is 150 metres high. And each chimney contains two flues. The power station was built during the '70s and '80s, like me and Western Barbie. Another fun fact: areas rich in coal also produce strong clay. Huntly brick is a distinctive light brown and yellow and used in the construction of many local buildings, including the presbytery.

*

One day at the presbytery, Granddad gave me a cardboard box full of monarch caterpillars. I dropped leaves into their box. The caterpillars ate slowly. Their yellow stripes flexed when they turned round corners. In the morning, I realised the caterpillars had escaped from the box. They were inching across the wild floral carpet. I couldn't see. I sat stranded on the edge of my bed looking at the doorway as though it was on the other side of the Waikato River; then I leapt and ran.

One caterpillar got squished under the heel of my foot. Later at school, I held a boy down in the playground and jumped on his chest because I knew he was keeping a secret from me. The school was throwing me a leaving party.

One road goes in to Huntly and one road goes out.

White crosses line State Highway 1 higgledy-piggledy, and the skins of hedgehogs wear the tracks of worn tires. At the edge of Huntly, on the summit of Taupiri Mountain, the graves of Māori monarchs rest in the sacred ground of the cemetery where Te Putu's pā once stood.

In my early twenties I passed through Huntly on InterCity buses and stared out at the dappled light on the Waikato River. I always looked for the Catholic church and the presbytery. The bus pulled in for refreshments at a place called The Pit Stop. The passengers climbed down from the bus as though they were stepping out to have a look at a rodeo. Inside: toilet breaks, pies, caramel squares, things with pink icing and tea. The other passengers were the God-fearing people of New Zealand, keepers of the working-class vigil, bearers of children. When we stopped in Huntly, time stopped. We all collected in the pocket of The Pit Stop like loose change.

*

In my early thirties on my first visit home from London, Mum and I packed up the car and went on a road trip. Mum drove, as I've never learned. I can't ride a horse either. We got on well during our road trip, except for when I said: 'Jesus Christ.'

'I don't understand why you have to take the Lord's name in vain.'

'It's just something I say when I'm surprised.'

'Well, why can't you say something else, like Elvis Presley?'

We stopped in Huntly at my request. There are photos of that journey too: me leaning against the door to the Catholic school, the light in my eyes, my long hair swept back. A shot of the presbytery: all that authentic Huntly brick. On the way out of town we took dual portraits in front of the Waikato River, the Huntly Power Station looming in the background like the Sphinx.

'You get over it,' Mum said, and I've always had a lot of respect for her point of view. Mum confessed that, at the age of 31, she had sometimes thought about jumping into the Waikato River. But then Mum realised she did still love my brother. We returned to Auckland and my grandparents helped us get set up in a flat.

Western Barbie saddled up Dallas and rode off into the sunset. Either that or she is packed away in a box. Mum still believes in God; I'm still lapsed. But when times are tough or I'm afraid, I pray. It's been a long time since my last confession. A shame, as I've always had a knack for it and these days my sins are better too. Sometimes, I'm still plagued by a lack of charity: I've thought bad things about my mother.

*

Spin me round and take my top off. There's a lever on my back. Push it and I just might wink, but only if I'm in the mood.

Joe Nunweek
Three Boys

Boy A wasn't even there when the deal went south. His friend Jayesh (more of an acquaintance, really) turned up at school with a foil ball of yellowing and stalky cannabis one morning. Jayesh exchanged part of it for $60 behind the windowless back of H Block with another kid, clandestine clouds of breath in the June air. The other kid wasn't as smart. 'I can get you all weed now, anytime,' he explained in a stage whisper to the kids in his row at second period. 'Jayesh is my supplier.'

The legend of the dealer acquaintance and his tactless would-be subcontractor travelled fast through Year 13. By the end of the day, they both had been caught red-handed, and the school fell into an enveloping reefer panic.

Bringing drugs to school is, and always has been, curtains. Students who get caught face near-certain suspension, then exclusion or expulsion. For students over the age of sixteen, it means they won't be coming back, most likely won't be able to attend conventional secondary education anywhere.

The school didn't stop there. They questioned the circle of friends, anyone who had seen a telltale glint of foil that day. They were all interviewed and told they needed to come forward with the names of any boy who was smoking dope at the weekend, at home – wherever.

First published on 24 November 2014 in *The Pantograph Punch*: pantograph-punch.com

Boy A's name was mentioned a number of times on the scrawled confess-all statements. And Boy A had inadvertently incriminated himself, though he didn't know it. For the past several months, he'd been seeing a school guidance counsellor for depression. In the sessions, he openly described having the same recreational alcohol and drug habits of virtually every eighteen-year-old boy in the country. The investigating vice-principal availed himself of the records, citing critical school safety reasons. He had his smoking gun.

Boy A was suspended immediately for a nebulous form of gross misconduct. He had done drugs, but he didn't do them at school, but he had done drugs with the boys who did do drugs at school. Plus, it was on the record.

Suspensions have to go before a disciplinary subcommittee of a school's Board of Trustees. Its members can choose between the school management's recommendation (generally, to exclude or expel the student), or they can reach an understanding that the kid comes back on certain conditions.

The student and their family are invited to attend the meetings and explain themselves. The meetings are not fun for anyone. School principals and vice-principals are asked how they can sleep at night. Board members with no legal background have to hold a student's future and the school's needs in their hands and hope they get the balance right.

Boy A's parents didn't have fun, either. Questioned on what they knew of his drug use, they spoke openly and honestly about how they let Boy A's friends gather at theirs and drink in the garage sometimes, because it was better to have a bunch of seventeen-year-olds wake up with blinding hangovers on a pool table than have them wander the streets at night or worse, climb into their Mitsubishi Mirages. Of course they snuck down to the garden for a toke, probably.

The parents were raked over the coals for it by the board and vice-principal alike. Did they know what they were doing was criminal? Did they want to explain that to the parents of the other young men? Then, the clincher: 'I can see where some of these attitudes to drugs and alcohol might be coming from.' Boy A's mother was set to leap over the table and hit someone, or walk out, or anything to stop the horrible mission drift of the investigation. Just who was on trial here? And what was it they'd done that broke the school's rules?

Amid the shouting match, Boy A's lay advocate, a recent law grad who had accompanied the family, eventually stammered out a few words about natural justice – pointing out that the parents' decisions weren't a relevant consideration, that the only reason anyone was in the room was that Boy A had chosen to be honest with an adult in the first place, and that if you wanted to make your school counselling service next to useless, the best message you could send to the students would be: 'We reserve the right to later use anything you say in confidence now against you later on.' This sounded more clumsy at the time than it does here – I know this, because the advocate was me.

Somewhere in the stammer, the message got through. Boy A, who had two terms of school left, who just needed to eke out enough credits to have a halfway decent choice of tech courses, would be allowed to return. He agreed to submit to a strict written behaviour agreement with the school, including random drug tests. If this still seems harsh rather than unlucky – if you know anything about teenage boys, peer pressure, how long THC stays in the system – then there's something else to know. In this system, you take what you can get.

Boy A was over sixteen, so if he had been expelled from school, no one else would have had to take him. If you disagree with the school board's decision, you can complain to the

Education Review Office, but they don't intervene lightly, and can't actually take any action to fix the situation beyond a report to the minister. Or you can go to New Zealand's nationwide Ombudsman, inundated with everything from Canterbury earthquake disputes to complaints about the withholding of free and publicly available data sets. If and when they get through their year-plus backlog, their powers are limited to a non-binding recommendation that schools don't have to follow.

Those are the free options. Boy A's parents – lots of parents – say they'll go to court if they need to. And they can, but a judicial review in the High Court of New Zealand costs between $25,000 and $30,000. It takes months if not years to go through the motions. At the end, with no guarantee of success, the student has still been out of school the whole time.

Lost time is not a currency that you can easily estimate and compensate, though no small amount of legal arithmetic goes into trying to do so. But as it passes by, it costs you dearly. If you miss a year of school at sixteen, you're paying it back at 26 – at 36 – beyond.

So if you think the school will drop its allegations, pop you straight back into class the next day, generally fall over to appease you for what would be a gross invasion of an adult's privacy, the shoe's on the other foot. The shoe is always on the other foot. A boy like you doesn't have parents that have a spare $25,000 lying around. And you don't have a spare two years.

Boy B didn't spend nearly a month in daily humiliation and bed-pissing terror just to get himself in trouble the first time he fought back. A classmate at the start of his fourth form year took an instant dislike to him, his weak, tense amicability, the way he couldn't throw a cricket ball. Boy B's bully was a head taller and could get him square in the nuts with a footy ball with an expertly placed kick, 20 metres out.

Usually he didn't bother with a show of skill when a swingeing whack in the back of the head with a maths textbook would do, or the pinprick agony of a compass in his shoulder, waiting for him to lean back. It was erratic – two, maybe three days at a time without. Somehow, that made it worse.

One afternoon at the start of maths, the bigger kid picked up a plastic chair. In a fluid arc worthy of *WWE SmackDown*, he brought it crashing down on Boy B's head. And in front of a class of thirty, Boy B spun around, pale limbs akimbo, and dealt the bigger kid one across the face.

It was a nasty hit for no training and no coordination. The bigger kid reeled with a bloody nose, a purple eye, a narrow gash from a wayward thumb. And then Boy B and his tormentor realised the teacher was about to come in, and they spontaneously did what they thought was a very clever thing to prevent things getting a lot worse for both of them. They marched to the school nurse and formulated a story on the five-minute walk. Boy B had been standing on a chair to change a light for Mr Stanton; it was stuck in the fitting and when it came loose with a jolt, he'd inadvertently elbowed his friend and classmate in the face. What do you expect when you get the most uncoordinated boy in the fourth form to carry out a menial task?

This seemed even more clumsy at the time than it does here. I know this, because Boy B was me.

My school had, and still has, a zero-tolerance approach to violence. Physical assault on another student falls under the category of 'gross misconduct' which can cop an immediate suspension, but neither I nor the other kid ended up excluded, let alone in front of a board. Perhaps there was some flicker of leniency because of the bullying aspect of it, or a weird 'law of the jungle' reluctance to intervene. They'd violently made their peace; let well enough alone.

More likely is the fact that we were each high-achieving students in the top stream for our year, with respectable extra-curricular involvement. We were also both (mostly) white.

As of 2013, New Zealand schools booted out around 3.7 times more boys than they did girls. That's predictable – the ethnic breakdown even more so. If you're Māori or Pasifika, you're between 30 and 60 per cent more likely to get expelled than your Pākehā counterparts. You find yourself in trouble more often at school until they kick you out. It's the beginning of a long and exceedingly expensive trail of over-representation.

Then you're at home, or somewhere, with no education and nothing to do, and you're finding yourself in trouble more often everywhere else. A 2001 UK study of 263 excluded young people found that 117 had no recorded offences prior to expulsion but offended later.* Conversely, only 14 had offended before being expelled and stayed clean afterward. So we know that getting kicked out of school doesn't serve as some short and sharp wake-up call, putting young adults on the straight and narrow.

And whether or not crime is a factor, there's an immediate effect on a student's life chances when they're removed from the secondary system. Our WINZ offices swell with the ranks

---

* David Berridge, Isabelle Brodie, John Pitts, David Porteous and Roger Tarling, 'The Independent Effects of Permanent Exclusion from School on the Offending Careers of Young People', *RDS Occasional Paper No. 71*, Research Development and Statistics Directorate, 2001: troublesofyouth.pbworks.com/f/occ71-exclusion.pdf

of the expelled – many of whom won't have attained a formal qualification, more of whom won't do anything after school.

The 2001 UK study painted the following picture:

> Permanent exclusion tended to trigger a complex chain of events which served to loosen the young person's affiliation and commitment to a conventional way of life. This important transition was characterised by . . . the loss of time structures, a re-casting of identity, a changed relationship with parents and siblings, the erosion of contact with pro-social peers and adults, a closer association with similarly situated young people and heightened vulnerability to police surveillance.

If we know a lot about what happens after a school expulsion, we don't know a great deal about how students have performed beforehand. Most students who get kicked out of school, I suspect, are neither troubled yet brilliant loners – blowing up the science lab or performing an elaborate prank on the teachers – nor would-be school shooters who need to be taken out of the system to protect themselves and others.

They're average-to-poor students and average-to-poor athletes with little extracurricular value to their college. And if there's no implicit assumption that they're a lost cause, there certainly isn't the counter-impetus to try to remain responsible for their management and welfare that might apply if they were a lot smarter, faster or stronger.

And assuming for a moment that you endorse zero-tolerance rules for otherwise tolerant schools, that you think that everyone who breaks the rules should be punished equally, there's a compounding unfairness to this. Because bright kids are usually better at breaking the rules and not getting caught.

Which is to say: we smoke our weed and sink our piss circumspectly, and we bully others to the brink of abject, desperate misery without leaving a trace you'll ever be able to find. When we're bored, and we're always bored, we'll egg on one of the less fortunate kids – the ones without self-control, who perform for attention, who are too impulsive for their own good – until they do something stupid and funny. And then we watch the fireworks from a safe distance.

If you're an educator, this is what at least some of your little stars do virtually every day of the week. You could redress the balance by redesigning school and everything around it, the internet included, as a sort of panopticon for teens. Chances are, you'd rather try to figure out something that doesn't involve monitoring them all, and that doesn't let those at the bottom of the heap cop the consequences.

Boy C was at a Wellington co-educational school, and sixteen, and lonely. Diagnosed with a double-whammy of ADHD and Asperger's, his record wasn't fantastic. It ran to several pages of late arrivals to class, getting out of his chair and wandering when he'd been told not to, of petty and poorly concealed thefts, of pulling hair or punching in the back when ignored or upset. He was too small for his age to do much harm, and honest to a fault when caught red-handed. And he was always caught, and so his list grew.

The school holidays after he turned sixteen were spent the way he usually spent them – under a sporadically adjusted sea of medication, feeling as though he didn't have a friend in the world. His parents relaxed the tough rules on devices and screen time they set to try to get him to focus on his homework during term time. He'd go on Facebook, live vicariously through the statuses and photos of classmates who never gave him the time of day during term. Then on the last day of holiday, he was added to a group chat. A bunch of guys and girls, and they were talking about sex.

They asked him if he'd ever done it.

yes

They didn't believe him, the jokes and the 'fuck offs' streaming into a blur. Who with? He had a flash of inspiration – and before his better judgement caught up, he'd typed in the name of his history teacher.

Suddenly, they were all interested, egging him on, asking for more details about when, the positions, what it was like. It felt good, typing, them laughing, wanting more. And then the next day they all showed Ms Shelton the history teacher the Facebook conversation and he was suspended.

At the Board of Trustees meeting, Boy C's parents were told he was facing expulsion for continual disobedience. The Ms Shelton affair had been the last straw – she would no longer have him in her class. For his parents, it was just another setback. They had both sacrificed pay and regular working hours to be at home with him as much as possible. They had worked with the school constantly and cooperatively.

For its part, the school had dug into its entitlements from the government for a while (New Zealand schools receive a Special Education Grant of non-individualised funding, which they can choose how to spend; individual students, with their parents' help, can apply for the Ongoing Resourcing Scheme, which secures things like teacher aides and help from specialists). But after the teacher aide who worked best with Boy C had to move on at the end of the previous school year, the funding lapsed.

Asked about what had happened to it at the meeting, both the vice-principal and board deflected. They were responsible for over a thousand students, and the funding was very limited. Not everything could be devoted to being one boy's keeper.

Towards the end, Boy C asked to read a statement he had prepared. It was probably the longest and most controlled speech he'd ever given, even as he trembled and focused on his handwritten refill. He was sorry for everything he'd done. He'd never had a girlfriend, or a friend, and he just wanted to keep being talked to and keep being included. He said he could try to explain how as the medication wore off he stopped thinking of consequences and just acted on impulse, but that he knew it wasn't an excuse. He said he just wanted to stay, that he would even do some days at home to avoid trouble. He wanted to finish NCEA Level 1 and then find a course somewhere. He just wanted one last chance.

The board took four minutes to decide that Boy C would be expelled. When they did, he hid his face behind his sheet of paper so they wouldn't see him burst into tears.

If Boy C's family had taken it further and sought a judicial review of the decision, there's a possibility the board's decision may have been overruled. In February, the High Court did the same for a student at Auckland's Green Bay High. His exclusion was found to be illegal, and there was a failure to take into account special recommendations or the opinion of a child psychologist before making the decision. But it's tens of thousands of dollars to get to that point. For someone with special educational needs, expulsion can be a marginalising, deeply isolating thing – for Boy C it was as if the last link with the normal warp and weft of daily life had suddenly been severed.

A sudden media focus on court reviews of BoT decisions earlier this year attracted the usual voices, some of them positively fascistic. Rent-a-quote parenting expert Nigel Latta gravely intoned that parents who invoked a civil right and brought lawyers into a Board of Trustees matter were 'wrong'. More usefully, law professor Bill Hodge pointed out that the community volunteers who act as administrators shouldn't have to go to bed wondering if they'll end up on the wrong side of a High Court judgment. The answer, as ever, is access.

Youthlaw's 2012 report Out of School, Out of Mind found that England, South Africa and certain provinces of Canada have an administrative structure in place for school exclusions to go to an independent appeal panel.* As a regime, it's faster and less costly for both school and family. It also hasn't had a floodgate effect – only a quarter of all appealed cases found in favour of the pupil. Even on those stats, more New Zealand students would be getting wrongful decisions overturned under such a system than are right now.

This sort of access isn't just about a vindicating day in court for protective mothers or fathers. The lower stakes could mean schools waste less time defending poor decisions than explaining their own poor circumstances. For its own part, without wearing the hat of school administrators, a panel could decide a matter on natural justice and not resource constraints.

In doing so, they'd send an implied message to the Ministry of Education: you're letting your schools down, and the effect is that they let their neediest down. It's no more activist than

---

* 'Out of School, Out of Mind: The Need for an Independent Education Review Tribunal', YouthLaw, 1 August 2012: youthlaw.co.nz/wp-content/uploads/Out-of-School-Out-of-Mind-web1.pdf

the tenor of certain recent High Court decisions, but it creates an affordable, fair middle ground between that forum and the stale biscuits and Bushells of a staffroom on a Wednesday night.

These kids are not political priorities, though their potential future cost suggests they should be. A similar panel in New Zealand is probably years down the track – and even if that's the case, the best schools and boards are already realising that youth misconduct and discipline are dynamic. Offenders and victims trade places on a dime, the worst behaviour is a symptom and not a disease, parents need empowering, and psychologists, social workers – even lawyers – have a part in facilitating a fair outcome. I've seen them do so, and they do it against fearful financial odds.

Some of the students that get in deep trouble this year will be enrolled at those schools, and will face those boards, and they'll be the lucky ones. But the expulsion process in New Zealand isn't always fair, and a lot of the time it can be final. Sometimes you squeak through, or sometimes you're too smart and too rich to have to squeak through in the first place. And sometimes you won't even be in with a chance. Sometimes never.

Certain details, including locations and names where used, have been changed to protect former students, their families, and those school staff and boards who do what they can in a bad system.

Matt Vickers
Lecretia's Choice

Half a World Away

Lecretia's most telling symptom, and the one she's struggled with the longest, is something called homonymous hemianopsia. It means that she is blind in one side of her field of vision. In her case, it's her left side.

It's an inconvenient affliction, but also a fascinating one, which reveals a little of the inner workings of the human brain. Lecretia's tumour is on her right-hand side but the contrariwise nature of the brain's hemispheres means that damage to the right-hand side of the brain affects the left-hand side of the body, and vice versa. There is nothing wrong with Lecretia's eyes. They are both in working order and she can see through either of them if the other is blocked. But her visual cortex is ravaged by cancer, so although a full picture is being passed through her optic nerve, her internal screen is only capable of processing the right-hand half of the image.

Lecretia Seales was diagnosed with brain cancer in 2011. On 20 March 2015, Lecretia and her lawyers filed a statement of claim with the High Court of New Zealand arguing that her GP should not be prosecuted under the Crimes Act 1961 for assisting her in her death with her consent, and that under the Bill of Rights Act 1962 she had the right to not be subjected to the unnecessary suffering of a long, cruel death.

Along the way, Lecretia's husband, Matt, maintained a blog, Lecretia's Choice (lecretia.org), where these pieces were first published on 28 April, 20 May and 31 May 2015.

What this means for her in practice is something called hemispatial neglect. In some ways, the left-hand side of her world doesn't exist for her. I notice that if people approach her on her left, and talk to her, she might ignore them altogether, even if she hears them perfectly well. When she walks around the house, she frequently bumps into things with the left side of her body, because she doesn't register the presence of objects in her path if they are on her left. You'd think a person with this condition would compensate, that having the knowledge that you aren't seeing your left side would mean you'd become conscious of that lack of awareness and you'd turn your head to pick up the things you were missing on your left. But in reality that doesn't happen. Lecretia's brain tricks her into thinking she is seeing everything she needs to see.

When we have dinner, she will eat the right-hand half of the food on her plate. When she's done, I reach across the table and turn her plate 180 degrees to reveal the half she's ignored, and then she eats that. Our cat has figured out exactly what's going on, and he will invariably approach Lecretia from her left side, and if I'm not quick enough, he'll successfully steal food from her without her noticing. When she reads a page, if she's not careful, she will often ignore the left-hand words and lose track of what she's reading. If she's looking at two columns of items, such as on a restaurant menu, she'll ignore the left column. And whenever she's lost something – she is forever losing things – usually it will be in front of her, on her left, and she just hasn't seen it. 'I don't have a fork,' is a common complaint at dinner. None of this was obvious before Lecretia's diagnosis, and if it had been a factor it would have been a much more subtle symptom than it is now.

In late 2010, when Lecretia was in good health, she was driving home alone one evening from a night class in Newlands.

The weather was terrible, it was dark, and as she approached a slight bend in the road, she hit a parked car on the left-hand side of her, totalling her car and doing a lot of damage to the other. She walked away shaken but unharmed. A nearby resident said it had happened before on that bend. I taxied out and picked her up from a good Samaritan's house on Newlands Road, and we took a taxi back home again, while our car was towed away.

As the days followed, we explained it away as a genuine accident. The conditions, the location, the fact it could have happened to anyone. We didn't look deeper, didn't see what else might have been right in front of us. I wish I had been more aware of what we might not have been seeing. Was it possible this was the first sign something wasn't right? We might have got Lecretia diagnosed sooner, got her treated sooner, got the whole damn thing resected. If I were a neurologist, I suppose, I might have noticed something was amiss. But I didn't notice, and here we are. And I know that now and for years to come, I will always wonder if things could have turned out differently, if I hadn't been so blind.

The Kindness of Strangers

I am sure that people who recommend obscure clinical trials or alternative treatments mean well. They think 'this could really help them!' and they only look at the possible upside. We might be grateful for the help, after all, for being pointed to something we might have overlooked. It's a long shot, but we just might save Lecretia's life, right?

But do those well-meaning people consider the work that puts on us and on Lecretia? Do they consider what happens if we follow it up and it doesn't help? That, if it were pursued, and it failed, we would hold a grudge against that person forever, for wasting what could have been quality time with a desperate, dying person on a false lead?

At this point, with Lecretia's time left so precious, we can only look at options that have a scientifically based track record of helping people with Lecretia's exact condition. We are terrified of Lecretia spending her remaining time in hospital through side effects and complications, which is the last thing she wants, but which is a real risk with trials and experimental therapies.

For example, a very intelligent and well-connected friend of mine reached out to me with an offer of help, without really knowing much about my wife's medical condition or current circumstances. He had a contact who had a PhD and had helped with 'all sorts of cancers'. His heart was in the right place, and I know he was only trying to help – after all, everyone wants Lecretia to live – but below is a letter I had to write him in response. I hope he doesn't mind me publishing it, because in part I would like to send it to everyone who sends me a link to an article on the internet, or a lead for a clinic in Germany or Russia, insisting that we have to follow it up. In most cases, if the option is any good, we have already investigated and dismissed it, or they either cannot help Lecretia or she is ineligible for their trial, or they have refused or ignored our pleas for compassionate admission.

Lecretia is already taking all the alternative supplements she can that have no or low risk of harming her. We have worked and continue to work hard for my wife, trying to balance reasonable health interventions with what her body will allow, while trying to maintain her quality of life. But more than that we are taking into account Lecretia's wishes and what she wants to do in terms of treatment. Her scope for exploring new approaches is very limited.

Dear friend,

My wife has suffered through surgery, radiotherapy and chemotherapy and is now confined to a wheelchair, losing her ability to focus, and her ability to see. She has entered palliative care because her oncology team believes nothing more can be done for her from an anti-cancer perspective. We have received second and third opinions, and they concur with that assessment. The expectation is that she has limited time to live.

Giving us false hope at this point would be extraordinarily cruel. We have been sent so many false leads, and we have some quite nasty people making us feel guilty because we aren't chasing their miracle cure fantasies. We are coming to terms with the implications of Lecretia's health, and making us feel guilty for accepting what is naturally and likely going to happen is just unkind. We are likely going to have to deal with the loss of someone we love deeply. Dealing with guilt too will just complicate and intensify our grief.

So I ask that if you do make a suggestion to me, you do not make me feel guilty if I turn down your help. Because my wife cannot travel, has no desire for further treatment that has little chance of working, and it would take an extraordinary opportunity to make us want to divert my wife from her current path of seeking quality of life from her remaining time on this Earth.

If your lead fails, and I expend money and time and effort on it, then that would be an enormous burden on you. You will have screwed over a grieving family. So before recommending anything, please consider whether you really want that responsibility? How confident are you that it'll work? On what basis? Medical knowledge and experience? The fact it worked with Lecretia's precise medical condition? An article you read? Did you evaluate the sources? Because that's what I'll have to do. I'll have to spend time poring through scientific articles to evaluate the chance it'll work for Lecretia, spend mental energy on a judgement call on whether it's worth putting everything on the line for, instead of spending time with her. Or is it just hearsay? A hunch?

We don't have time for 'it might work' or 'what have you got to lose'. We could lose everything. We could lose our last remaining precious moments with Lecretia. That is what is at stake. We only really have time for certainty.

I get recommendations all the time from unqualified strangers, and I can dismiss those. Dismissing a recommendation from a person I respect is a harder thing to do – and I hate to do it. So please be careful and think hard before putting me in that position.

I am sorry for being so blunt with you. But I worry that you may not appreciate the enormity of our personal situation and how involving yourself in the way you propose might affect our relationship, which I value greatly.

As a result, my friend replied that he would follow up with his lead and qualify it before coming to me with it. He has changed tactics from putting the work on me to doing the work himself to really evaluate what he is proposing and whether it can help Lecretia in particular. I'm utterly grateful for that.

If you're the sort of person to recommend medical treatments to strangers with the intent of trying to help, and I don't mean just Lecretia, I mean to anyone who is facing a terminal illness, my advice would be to do the same. Be sceptical. What is the science? Do you really have the skills to evaluate the science? Is there any science at all? How many failure stories sit behind the success stories? Have you qualified the truth of the success stories? How similar are the circumstances to the person you are trying to help? And if this is so successful, why hasn't it been peer-reviewed? Why hasn't it been adopted by the oncology community? Why isn't it part of the standard of care? It costs you nothing to send a link, but it can cost a family a lot to receive it if it isn't qualified and its veracity and relevance evaluated. Please don't put the work on the family. They just don't have the time.

If you want to advocate a treatment, I'd suggest that the right approach is to lobby the scientific community to evaluate and peer-review it, rather than pushing it on to desperate families who are already agonising over every medical decision.

We want to imagine that all cancer is treatable. That we can always beat it. That there is always an answer. The statistics tells us that that is just not true, and that is the sad reality. Lecretia hasn't given up yet, and she has no desire to die, but she is facing very tough odds. We have to be very careful about next steps, so that we can give her the best possible outcome, without putting what she has left at too much risk.

Hospital Bed

On Friday morning, less than two days after the end of Lecretia's hearing, we woke and began the task of getting Lecretia out of bed to begin her morning routine. However, despite being awake and lucid, her paralysis had taken a firm grip on her whole body, and she had become as rigid as a plank, unable to bend at the waist. Her brother and I worked to lift her together, and almost had to force her to bend so that she could get into a seated position.

We took delivery of a hoist that morning but when the hospice doctor saw Lecretia at lunchtime, he said that what she really needed was a hospital bed. This was duly organised, but coming into the long weekend meant that the delivery driver got his message late in the day and no doubt had plans for the weekend other than answering calls and driving a bed all the way back to us from the Hutt Valley.

Further calls to the delivery company on Saturday morning were fruitless. One of the nurses, sharing our frustration, went above and beyond and organised for us to be able to pick up a bed from the hospital if we could organise our own transport. If that hadn't have happened, I have no doubt we would have ended up with Lecretia needing to be moved out of her home – against her wishes – and into either the hospital or the hospice via ambulance so that she could be comfortable. Lecretia's friend Angela helped me and her brother Jeremy pick up the bed and put it in the back of her SUV. Once it arrived, it took a good hour to figure out how to put it together.

Thankfully, by early Saturday evening, and through the generosity of the district nurses pulling strings on a long weekend, we had Lecretia settled in a hospital bed in our living room, able to be elevated or moved to her side and so on.

I am not relaying these facts to be critical. I am hugely grateful that between the hospice, the DHB and ourselves we were able to work together to get a good result for Lecretia, but I have to admit it was pretty stressful. It would have been a struggle for someone without Lecretia's strong support network.

Lecretia is not well. Her eyes are closed most of the time. She is having trouble swallowing. She is talking less and less. But she is facing all of this without complaint. She says she has no pain, and she has not taken any painkillers. This morning she ate feijoas, like the ones from her parents' home in Tauranga. She is lying in her bed with a quilt sewn for her by a friend who worked with her at the Law Commission. Our cat, Ferdinand, has been sharing her bed with her, laying in her lap, or at the end of the bed.

I've been holding her hand and talking about holidays we've taken together. Things we've seen and done and food we've eaten. One of her favourite memories was floating in the lagoon at Aitutaki in the Cook Islands. I describe it to her: the sand, the smell of sunscreen, the salt in the air, the warmth of the sun and the water. The sense of our time there being lazy and long and as vast as an ocean. It makes her smile.

Sometimes she says to me, 'Let's go.' I'll ask where and she'll say, 'Anywhere.' She wants me to get her in the car and start driving. As though her illness is tied to this place and that if we got far enough away from it she could cast it off like a veil. I wish that were true.

Every so often a tremor comes. Her whole body shakes and vibrates. The pressure of the tumour on her brain stem is causing her brain to reconfigure, to shift against itself like restless earth, causing her body to tremble, the frame of the bed shaking and rattling. And then it subsides, and she rests.

Lecretia's choice is imminent, and we don't know yet if she will get to make it. She's been through a few things already that she would rather not have had to go through, but she has taken all of this in her stride and with as much grace and dignity as she can muster. Would she have chosen to go already if she'd had the choice? Surrounded by love and support like she has been, I doubt it. But she doesn't know what is yet to come, and what she will have to endure, and that must be terrifying. I know that having the ability to make a choice about how her life ends would give her more strength to face it.

It scares me that in not having the choice she had to consider suicide because she had no certainty or control as she headed into the unknown. Because these moments we are having now are so precious and we would have lost them. I feel for those families who have lost loved ones early because those loved ones weren't allowed to have the death they wanted.

She is facing this as she faces all things: with tremendous bravery and courage. I am so proud of her. I love her so much. I don't know what she will ultimately choose, or even whether she will get to. But for Lecretia, it was always having the choice that mattered, not the choice itself. We are hoping for a judgment that acknowledges and respects Lecretia's free will and autonomy over her own life; the ability to decide how she lives it and how it ends. That is all she wants.

Lecretia passed away from the symptoms of her brain cancer on 5 June, on the same day the High Court judgment in Seales v Attorney General was released to the New Zealand public. Although Lecretia did not achieve the rulings she sought, the judge agreed Lecretia's wishes were a rational and reasonable response to her circumstances, that she was not vulnerable or at risk of coercion, and that her autonomy should be respected and upheld. However the judge declared that although the logic and dignity of Lecretia's choice was hard to refute, New Zealand law did not accommodate the interpretation Lecretia wanted, and that only Parliament could change the law to allow terminally ill patients such choices. Lecretia's case, along with a Voluntary Euthanasia Society petition, compelled Parliament to take the issue of assisted dying to select committee for review, something that has never happened before in New Zealand political history, despite private members' bills being presented to the house in 1995 and 2003. At the time of publication, the select committee inquiry is still ongoing.

Rachel Buchanan
For the Trees

In mid-2014, photographer Ann Shelton wrote to me, asking if I wanted to contribute a piece for a special issue of Enjoy Public Art Gallery's occasional online journal. The theme was trees.

Shelton suggested I might like to do something on momori rākau, the rare carved trees out by the harbour heads in Wellington. I was chuffed to be asked but my first thought was no, absolutely not.

I had written about these trees once before for a memory studies journal; it had not been an especially positive experience.

That article, 'Re-making Memory on Matiu and Other "Settlement" Sites', which was published in an online academic journal, documented my attempts to engage with the eighteen sites handed back to Taranaki Whānui ki Te Ūpoko o Te Ika in a 2009 Treaty settlement.

In 2010, my daughter, my niece, my father, my mother and my brother had come with me on various pilgrimages to each place. The best-known settlement site was Matiu, the island in Wellington harbour. It's good out there but it can also feel desolate and damaged, especially around the old quarantine station near the summit.

But Matiu was paradise compared with many of the other settlement sites. The empty Wainuiomata secondary school

First published in 2015 in *The Dendromaniac*, an Enjoy Occasional Journal: journal.enjoy.org.nz had the torn aura of the apocalypse. One block had recently been burned. Many more were tagged or boarded up.

The Wi Tako Scenic Reserve was worse. A Department of Conservation sign warned: *Please do not enter this reserve because dead pines are a significant hazard.*

Lake Kōhangapiripiri and Lake Kōhangatera – better known as Pencarrow Lakes – appeared equally bleak. To get there, we drove through Eastbourne, unlocked Burdan's Gate, and kept on going towards the harbour heads. To our left, the hills blazed with gorse; to our right the sea burned a brilliant blue. The skeletons of dead boats and docks listed on the wide, pebbly shore. A concrete platform fingered the sea. *Danger Sewage Outfall*, the sign said. *The sea in this area is polluted. Do not swim, take fish, or shellfish.*

We wanted to visit the dendroglyphs (*dendro*, a Greek word element meaning tree and *glyph*, a carving). Apparently, there were three by the lakes. These engraved trees were once common on Rēkohu (the Chatham Islands) but they are now endangered. These three near Wellington are the only ones on the mainland.

We parked the car and Dad led the way up a steep path. My brother Ben and I panted along after him. From the crest, we could see the lakes, two grey eyeballs in a blasted face. We saw flax, toetoe and gorse but no trees. There was barely any scrub. We climbed up higher, towards the 1866 Pencarrow lighthouse. By now, the hills were quite bald.

Was this a joke? It felt like a joke.

I suggested we try some flat land, away from the wind, and we took the path that went towards swampy wetlands. We skirted some water then rounded a corner. There was a rickety fence and . . . a tree! Just one. Could this be it? I had expected something enormous, a towering giant with a wide girth as a canvas, but this karaka tree was gnarled and modest, shaped by the winds into a flat-topped green flag flying east. Its leaves shone a glossy, deep green.

Dad could not climb the low fence – or would not – but Ben and I did.

We stared at the grey trunk. It was lumpy and indented but hard to read, like skin when a tattoo has been removed. Because we didn't know what to expect, we didn't know what to look for.

'I can see some shapes,' Ben said. 'I think this is it. There is a bird. And a tiki I think.'

I read later that the carving depicts a fish.

Did the carver want to communicate with his contemporaries, or with his descendants – with people like my brother and me? Or did he work purely for himself, caught up in his own audacity and skill? He cut his marks into a living tree. He cut into the bark, gently, not going so deep that he would damage the living tissue of the tree. He wanted to leave the soft, living body beneath his canvas intact. The technique was as much etching or engraving as carving.

The tree was a historical marker with a fence but no sign. How come it was here, the only tree at the lake? Was it always the only tree here or was there once a small forest of compact, twisting trees, curling themselves around the wind, their trunks sheltered by flax and fern? I felt protective of the tree, its modesty and its singularity, the quiet mystery it invoked through the oblique statements knifed in its side. I wanted the site to stay as it is – hard to find and remote, so understated.

Although Dad did not actually see the carving, he saw the tree and he was there with us. We spent the day together. That was enough. That was the value.

But the warmth of that day, the closeness I had enjoyed with my dad and with Ben, all those good memories had been subsequently smothered by the peer reviewing and revision process. It made my writing cold. I loathed the pedantry of the footnoting conventions and the queries about the most minor of historical facts. It was a waste of time yet it was my job. I was an academic. I had to write scholarly essays. I had to follow the conventions. We all did.

My article was published online some time in 2011. By then, I could barely stand to look at it.

My patience with this sort of work was almost gone. The chaos of my home life sapped what little tolerance I had left.

In the first six months of 2011, it had appeared that two of the people I loved most would soon die.

My mother had been diagnosed with dementia and then she had collapsed in church. 'Massive stroke,' Dad said. I couldn't go back to New Zealand to be with her because my partner was sick. Eye roll. I thought it was a bad case of man flu. I'd reluctantly driven him to hospital. The closer we got, the sicker he appeared. His skin was grey and he could not speak because of the pain. They rushed him through to a bed. The nurses and doctors took off his shirt and put the sticky pads on his chest, like the ones you see on TV. I watched, useless and shocked. They thought he was having a heart attack. Pain ripped across his upper arm and shoulder. Two whacks of morphine did nothing. After several hours of drama, it was discovered that Mike had pneumonia. 'The devil's claw' is medical slang for the pain that can be referred from a chronically infected lung to a shoulder. He was on IV antibiotics for three days and in bed for two weeks. His strength was gone. He was scared and quiet but at least he did not smoke anymore.

I had to do everything at home. Our three girls were then aged five, six and nine. I also kept commuting out to work at

La Trobe University where I was a lecturer in the journalism programme. The university was a convenient 50 kilometres or so away.

Meanwhile, the emails about the 'Re-making Memory' article piled up. Files were attached, marked with those maddening track-change bubbles. The editors were just doing their job. The problem was with me. Everything was collapsing.

In May 2011, Fairfax announced more redundancies at its newspapers. Sub-editing would be outsourced. I stared out my office window at the trees. It was autumn and I saw the leaves had turned a deep yellow. The sun shone through them, lighting them up. The beauty of those leaves astonished me and some of that warm yellow light entered my brain. I could not go on teaching a vocational course when the vocation was disappearing. None of the justifications worked anymore. My mind had been stripped of its protective barrier. I had no bark, only bite. I wrote a hot-headed letter to the head of school explaining that I would not be able to teach journalism in semester 2. It was not a resignation; it was more of a plea for release. I tried to negotiate a transfer to the history department but I failed.

Three months later, I was unemployed. That phase of my life as an academic was over.

I finished in the August. By the following January, I was back in New Zealand, living in a rented house in Lyall Bay and looking for work. So was Mike. Our children were at primary school up the road.

We spent all of 2012 in Wellington. I immersed myself in the intrigues of the Taranaki Māori world. I no longer thought of the Treaty settlement as a positive thing. Perhaps I never had in the first place. Most of the money appeared to have gone. Meanwhile, the Serious Fraud Office had announced an investigation into transactions connected with the Wellington

Tenths Trust, a body that represents Māori land-owners in the capital. Furthermore, the Office of Treaty Settlements had offered another iwi some settlement sites in the middle of town, just along the way from where our tūpuna had lived at Te Aro Pā. It was a mess – but like any soap opera, pretty compelling too.

When Ann Shelton got in touch in 2014, I dug out the 'Re-making Memory' article. The year living in Wellington had changed my opinion of it. I was reaching towards something, certainly, but my knowledge had been incomplete. The conclusion was cringeworthy. I had suggested that the eighteen Treaty settlement sites were re-stoking Taranaki Whānui fires of occupation around the harbour. This was now so untrue as to be laughable.

I aim, in all my writing about the Taranaki Māori world, to turn things around, to find the good in the bad, but in this case, my strategy had flopped.

But there was *some* good stuff in the essay. It was still worth sharing. I sent Ann a link and explained that, sorry, I had nothing else to say about the carved trees. In fact, I had nothing to say about any trees at all. I knew nothing about them. Not my field. Not my thing. No money in it. Not an academic anymore. Not an artist either. Had no time. Had another book to get on with. Had to stop doing unpaid work.

Yet, here I am, writing for free again. Ann's invitation has started something new for me, something important, even if I don't yet understand exactly what or why.

In *Six Memos for the Next Millennium*, Italo Calvino considers what a work of literature would be like if it was 'conceived outside the *self*'. Such a work, he writes, would allow writers to 'not only enter into selves like our own but to give speech to that which has no language, to the bird perching

on the edge of the gutter, to the tree in the spring and the tree
in the fall, to stone, to cement, to plastic . . . .'

As I write, it is spring in Melbourne, where we live once
more. Three weeks ago, the fig tree by our bedroom window
was speckled with the tiniest green buds. Now the tips of its
branches are crowned with vigorous new leaves. I can even see
figs up the top, pale green and hard as rock. Soon they will
be ripe and we will be woken by the sound of fruit bats and
possums gorging on them and the next morning the deck
will be sticky with half-chewed figs, the remnants of their
midnight feast.

Last night, Melbourne was lashed by a storm. Lightning
took out some signalling points at Flinders Street station.
Hundreds of trains were cancelled. Lighting struck a house in
Prahran and it caught on fire. At 2 a.m., I ran outside to shut
the windows in my writing room. Papers and photos were all
at risk of a fine soaking. Mission accomplished, I went back
to bed and listened to the thunder roar above us. I had never
heard anything like it. The sound was rich, luxuriant and
menacing. Lightning x-rayed our room. The dog went ape.
The children stood in the hallway, their hair stuck to the sides
of their faces. 'The light is scratching the sky,' the oldest one
had said the first time she watched a storm.

There was more lightning and thunder at 6 a.m. Mike
reminded me how his friend Danny had seen someone struck.
'They were at school. The lightning hit a tree and it went down
into the ground and then up into Danny's friend. It lifted him
up and all his clothes came off.'

'What do you mean?'

'They were just gone, his clothes. Incinerated.'

'Did he die?'

'Yes, he died.'

Naked and spinning, catapulted through the air by the purest of light; a flash of insight can feel as radical as that.

Although I had initially said no to Ann, I continued to think about her invitation and about trees and eventually these thoughts meshed together and – quite suddenly – I saw that trees and forests had been central to my work, especially in these past few years.

In 2012, I had started a new research project on a piece of Māori land owned by our whānau. I had no funding, no outcome in mind. I just wanted to know more about this mysterious block, Orimupiko 22 at Ōpunake, a small town on Taranaki's spectacular Surf Coast highway. I took a trip up there with Dad and my youngest child. I've documented this journey elsewhere but the thing I had forgotten – or over-looked somehow – when Ann got in touch was the buried forest that we found. It was extraordinary.

Whenever the farmer went to dig a ditch or lay a drain he'd hit trees, big, black rātā logs all pointing in the same direction: seawards. 'If you dig down deep enough, you'll find natives,' he told us. I interviewed a volcanologist who had mapped all the soil around there and learned that the mountain, Taranaki, felled the forest 7000 years ago. A portion of his summit collapsed and the volcanic debris spewed down the side, destroying everything in its way. The trees were buried under 5 metres of ash, stone and gravel. The world was upside down. Cows chewed grass grown from volcanic soil that had come from the heart of the mountain. A forest existed under the earth. It was being excavated and burnt, destroyed for a second time, or so it seemed.

The trees were coming for me. I encountered another buried forest later that year: the forest that made newspapers. For the past 26 years, my stories and headlines had been published in

newspapers, but I had never given a thought to the paper itself
and how it was made. That was about to change.

A few months after I saw the remnants of the 7000-year-old
forest beneath our land in Taranaki, I started work as an off-
shored sub-editor for Fairfax, the Australian-owned company
that publishes many New Zealand newspapers, including
Wellington's *Dominion Post* and *The Press* in Christchurch.
Our crew subbed regional Australian papers from a basement
in Boulcott Street, Wellington. I decided to write about what
I was doing and to research the implications of the collapse
in newspaper manufacturing. Paper-making was one of the
industries in catastrophic decline. I read that Norske Skog
was going to close the number-two paper machine at its mill
in Kawerau. The Norwegian multinational would cut newsprint production by 150,000 tonnes and more than a hundred
people would lose their jobs. I negotiated access just before
the machine was shut.

The mill had opened in 1955, right next to the raw material it
needed – the pine forests of the central North Island. Returned
soldiers started planting the trees in 1919. In the Depression,
men dug in trees too. By the end of the 1930s, Kāingaroa was
the biggest manmade forest in the world.

At its peak in the early 1970s, the Kawerau paper mill and
its sister kraft mill next door employed 2000 people. Only a
decade ago, 600 people still worked on the three paper-making
machines. By January 2013, there were 170 people left.

As well as newsprint, Kawerau used to make book paper
at the mill too. The last book run made the paper for the
Australasian editions of the *Twilight* books.

The title of the bestselling series of vampire books is
horribly apt. Within five years – probably less – I think the
mill will shut altogether. The talk, now, is of using the trees for

biofuel. The forests, according to one report, could be New Zealand's new oilfields.

Now another forest has arrived in my life. This one – just ten minutes from my front door in Altona, a western suburb of Melbourne – comprises 6000 trees: red gums; paper barks; and she-oaks, planted by New York-based land artist Agnes Denes in 1998.

I heard about Denes' *Forest for Australia* a week after I told Ann Shelton that I could not write anything about trees.

Agnes Denes' best-known work is *Wheatfield – A Confront- ation* (1982). Denes got hold of two acres of abandoned landfill in Manhattan (on the site that is now Battery Park). She cleared it and planted a field of wheat. More than a thousand pounds of wheat was harvested and became part of 'End of World Hunger', an international art show. Seeds from the Manhattan crop were planted at twenty places around the world.

Much of Denes' practice has been with trees, in projects such as *Rice/Tree/Burial (Chaining the Forest)* from 1977 and her monumental work in Finland, where Denes made a mountain on which 11,000 people planted 11,000 trees.

I was intrigued, and decided to do a bit of digging to learn more about the Altona project. What happened next is a story for another time, but I am now in a conversation with Denes herself. I had a new message from her this morning about photographs of her forest here in Altona. I have already taken some but she wants more.

No, I can't write about trees. I know nothing about them. Not my field. Not my thing. No money in it. Not an academic anymore. Not an artist either. Have no time. Have another book to get on with. Have to stop doing unpaid work.

Next week, I visit the Agnes Denes forest again. A tree expert is coming with me.

Giovanni Tiso
Philemon and Baucis

For my parents, who have been reunited.

Two ordinary-looking trees, an oak and a linden, growing side
by side on a small hill, surrounded by a wall. But first, a tale of
two gods wandering in peasant disguise, seeking hospitality in
the homes of strangers, only to find *mille domos adiere locum
requiemque petentes, mille domos clausere serae*: a thousand
doors remain shut to their pleas. Until the gods reach the last
house in the town, where an old couple live in freedom-giving
poverty, each owing obedience only to the other. They take in
the strangers, and the poet minutely and tenderly describes
the table they set and the dinner they prepare, sharing the best
of what little they have. The reviving of the fire from the day
before, with leaves and dry bark. The cutting of a slice of an
old piece of bacon, softened in water and washed of its salt.
And then each of the courses, modest but proper and carefully
laid out, accompanied with wine. Above all, *vultus accessere
boni nec iners pauperque voluntas*: welcoming looks, and a
warm, solicitous disposition towards the uninvited guests.

Thus begins the story of Philemon and Baucis, as told by
Ovid in the *Metamorphoses*. Its original source, if any, is
unknown, although there is a biblical echo in what happens
next, as the gods reveal themselves to the mortals – by

First published on 26 May 2014 on Giovanni's blog Bat, Bean, Beam:
bat-bean-beam.blogspot.co.nz

magically increasing the supply of wine – and announce that they are about to lay waste to the town for the impiety of its inhabitants. Only the old couple will be spared, so long as they march to the top of the hill, without looking back. When they reach the summit and turn their 'no more forbidden eyes' (as per John Dryden's liberal translation), Philemon and Baucis see that the town has been drowned in a lake of sludge. While weeping for the loss of lives they watch their old home, which was *parva duobus* – barely enough for two people – be transformed into a temple, with marble floors and columns sprouting like vegetation in a forest. Whereupon Jupiter asks the couple to declare their wish, which the gods will grant.

The story is all in the next two lines. *Cum Baucide pauca locutus iudicium superis aperit commune Philemon*: after consulting briefly with Baucis, Philemon tells the gods their shared desire.

They didn't have to speak for long: their mind was already made up. Their wish had always existed, waiting for two passing gods to come along and fulfil it.

This is the part that has no biblical echoes whatsoever – it is all about earthly love, not the divine – and that my mother used to speak about with longing. The part where Philemon and Baucis ask to serve as priests in the newly erected temple, but above all that when their hour comes they be allowed to die together. *Nec coniugis umquam busta meae videam, neu sim tumulandus ab illa*: that she may not have to see my grave, nor I have to bury her.

When a loved one dies, it always feels as if death has just been invented. But Philemon and Baucis are the last people: by which I mean to each other, a state expressed by heavy-handed metaphor through the massacre of the rest of the townsfolk. And if there is no one else, if they are the last loved ones, to each be spared the death of the other is the ultimate gift: the promise to live their remaining years free of the fear of that pain.

When the time comes, the gods' design reveals itself in poetic form. The couple are sitting on the temple's foreground, reminiscing about what came to pass, when

> . . . *frondere Philemona Baucis,*
> *Baucida conspexit senior frondere Philemon.*
> *iamque super geminos crescente cacumine vultus*
> *mutua, dum licuit, reddebant dicta 'vale' que*
> *'o coniunx' dixere simul, simul abdita texit*
> *ora frutex . . .*

Frondere, what a magnificent verb: it means that the two have started to grow branches and leaves. And then 'farewell', 'oh, my spouse' they have time to say to each other before bark seals their mouths and the swift metamorphosis is complete.

Two ordinary-looking trees, an oak and a linden, growing side by side on a small hill, surrounded by a wall. What fate could be more sweet?

Elizabeth Knox

Thoughts Upon Watching People Shout People Down

I began writing this in October 2014 in response to one 'storm on Twitter' and finished it today, prompted by another.

I've been wondering whether, in most people, the instinct for agreement is stronger than the one for self-expression. When people agree they belong. And belonging doesn't necessarily mean feeling yourself part of a larger society. Quite often it can mean defining yourself in opposition to something that you perceive to be the large society – 'mainstream' this or that. How do we agree? Not by discussion so much as quickly letting other people know what we think, or by a kind of rushed calibration where we can discover what it is we should think, what our position should be. Agreements are established through the tone taken and the language used. Particular words and phrases. Saying things in a correct and unexceptional way. Each agreement has its own personality, its way of talking – its creep or swagger.

That urge to agree, to find out what the group thinks, to pacify and calm the most emotional individuals, to stand in the tree tops and shake our fists and make enough noise so that the lions, those lazy, maybe hungry lions out there, won't come too close – these instincts are all deeply human,

First published on 31 January 2015 on Elizabeth's blog Knoxon: elizabethknox.com/knoxon and calculated for survival. I never have any quarrel with what's deeply human. But these behaviours and instincts, the twitches and fends, the loving gestures, don't necessarily add up to a total unifying good.

What we have now with the internet is, I think, a much more heightened tendency to agreement, disguised as self-expression. Pure self-expression doesn't look like agreement. Not that it's oppositional, it just has a different voice. Someone you can hear maybe from further off, at the other side of the room, a little out of the light, further from the fire and lamps, closer to the light of the window – like Jane Eyre hiding behind the curtains and reading a book about British birds. Maybe that someone has their back to you, perhaps they're walking away. But is walking away necessarily dissent or opposition? Maybe they're just going for a walk, and doing a bit of thinking.

When we read deeply, openly, we are always meeting our fates on paper. I am sitting on a train reading an essay in a journal, or a book. I'm partaking of someone else's world view or wily seduction. And when I lay the book down, bent over my knee, I don't do anything else but think. Reading is like walking with wind and birdsong brushing my ears. I know I'm myself because the moment has made a bowl for me to curl up in, cool and sheltered. I'm reflecting on what I've read and that's somehow an equivalent to physical exercise, to walking along the tideline, swinging my arms. Sensation, movement, timeliness.

We used to walk to the train, the field, the village, the market, the foundry. We used to walk to visit the invalids of our father's parish, or to the shady stone *laverie* to wash our clothes. At some point we were all natural athletes. We were in our bodies and they were in space. We were natural readers too: fit, patient, habitual. (Although my 'we' never included everybody, since even when things were near their best, and the horizons of possibility for human life the farthest away they ever got, there were people without books or learning, or jobs, shelter, sustenance.) But we weren't always logged in and checking to see whether we still exist. It's like we're in a bar, morning, noon and night, with only bottles between ourselves and the mirror behind the bar. The lights are low and the mirror makes the room look big, but it's only an illusion of scale. Don't you long to lose sight of yourself?

The storm on the internet

If they're feeling alarmed, what is it that's alarming them: the situation, or the talk about the situation? The story they heard. The scary story they heard, and the other frightened people. Or are they enjoying their fear? Is their fear making them feel alive? Are they enjoying their anger? Is their anger (indignation, disapproval) making them feel large and consequential?

When I feel threatened or angered by something I read on the internet, I try to wait for that moment when I feel something apart from all the voices; something apart from *myself*, the aggregation of my history and hopes and desires for the future, and all the things I cling to to protect my ego, the face in the mirror behind the bar. I believe that if we hold ourselves in an undecided and even contradictory state, then there sometimes comes a moment that can teach us a truer relation to the world.

One thing that comes back to me as I write is a sound, the stumbling buzz of an invisible bumblebee in the lavender bush by our front door, just before dawn, summer, the 12th of January 2001. My mother, my sister Sara and I were returning from the hospital after Dad had died. The silence of the street, the silence of the house, Jack asleep, Fergus up waiting, and then a first sign of life after death, the stumbling buzz of an invisible early bumblebee in the lavender bush. When I think about that I am like one of those saints in the old paintings where the saint is his study, and on his desk is a human skull, a *memento mori*, a reminder of death.

We *should* be reminded of death. But usually we're only being reminded of danger. People have it in for us, somebody is going to kill us, there are those out there who hate us or what we hold dear. We get that all the time. We get what we can do to disguise the appearance that our lives are short. But what we need is the quiet study and the skull on the desk. We need to know that we will die, and that we owe something to our lives, and it must be something vital. Those lovely villains in old movies, the articulate Machiavellian ones, might say to the queasy heroine that 'Hate is vital and warming' – but the spectacle of people agreeing to hate isn't of life, it's the already bony thing, it's the same words being used, having to be used, like a catechism; the same phrases, as if *that's* self-expression.

Go back into the quiet room, the room empty of everyone but yourself. Go for a walk. Stand still and stare at something inhuman and alive, or inanimate and kinetic, like a river. Be with yourself and think, 'Who am I apart from all this? What is the world to me? What is my life to me?' Put out your hand and touch the top of the skull and think about life, what a short time there is in which to be yourself – your good self – and do good.

About the Contributors

Charles Anderson is a Nelson-based journalist whose work has appeared in the *International New York Times*, the *Guardian* and *National Geographic Traveller*. He won the 2015 Newspaper Feature Writer of the Year at the Canon Media Awards and the 2014 award for Innovation in Multimedia Storytelling for 'Lost in the Long White Cloud' (lostplane.co.nz), an interactive longform feature. He has worked in Thailand, Somalia, Indonesia, East Timor and India covering everything from food crises and peace-keeping to sex trafficking and cricket. He was named Cathay Pacific Travel Writer of the Year in 2012. He has worked across the Fairfax Media group but is now back reporting for the *Nelson Mail*, where he started his career.

Vicki Anderson is a solo mum of four beautiful children. A music journalist for more than ten years, she is currently the Arts and Entertainment editor at Fairfax newspaper *The Press* in Christchurch. She enjoys live music and collects records, art deco objects and stray animals. She dreams of one day writing a book that someone might want to read and thus ending the need to commute by bus.

Naomi Arnold is an award-winning journalist and editor who free-lances for a range of national and international magazines and newspapers including *Metro*, *North & South*, BBC.com and the *Sunday Star-Times*. She studied English and journalism at Otago and Canterbury, and now lives in Nelson with her partner Doug. She runs Featured (featured.org.nz), which collects great New Zealand nonfiction. She's online at naomiarnold.co.nz

Steve Braunias is the author of seven books, including *Civilisation* (Awa Press), which won the 2013 New Zealand Post Award for Nonfiction, and the surprise bestseller at Christmas 2014, *Madmen*

(Luncheon Sausage Books). His latest book, *Scene of the Crime* (HarperCollins), is a true-crime collection. He works for the *New Zealand Herald*.

Rachel Buchanan (Taranaki, Te Āti Awa) wrote *Stop Press: The Last Days of Newspapers* (Scribe, 2013) and *The Parihaka Album: Lest we Forget* (Huia, 2009). Her work on Taranaki has been published in *Te Pouhere Kōrero* (2012), *Australian Humanities Review* (2012) and elsewhere. In August 2015, she helped local children replant trees at Agnes Denes' *A Forest for Australia*, the first steps in the restoration of this major piece of conceptual art.

Kate Camp is the author of five collections of poetry from Victoria University Press. *The Mirror of Simple Annihilated Souls* won the 2011 New Zealand Post Book Award for poetry. Her most recent collection, *Snow White's Coffin*, was written during her time on the Creative New Zealand Berlin Writer's Residency. Kate is also the voice of Kate's Klassics, monthly radio conversations on classic books with Kim Hill. She lives in Wellington and works at Te Papa Tongarewa.

Megan Dunn graduated from Elam School of Fine Arts; in the late 1990s she was co-director of the artist-run space Fiat Lux in Auckland. In 2006 she completed her Masters in Creative Writing at the University of East Anglia and won an Escalator award from the New Writing Partnership (now The Writers' Centre Norwich). She currently lives in Wellington and her writing and art reviews have been published in *Art News*, *Circuit*, *Eyecontact*, the *New Zealand Listener*, *Metro* and *The Pantograph Punch*. Her first book, *Tinderbox*, is an irreverent inside take on chain bookselling and will be published by Galley Beggar Press in 2016. More info at davidhigham.co.uk/clients/Megan_Dunn.htm

Dan Eichblatt, a University of Auckland graduate, is a high school English teacher in Auckland. He runs his school's PSSP (Peer Sexuality Support Program) and recently started an LGBT+

support group for students. He has had two pieces of writing published in *Impolitikal*.

David Fisher started as a journalist in 1989 and has worked in community, provincial and national newspapers in New Zealand and abroad. He has won a number of journalism awards, twice been named New Zealand's Reporter of the Year and been made a Press Fellow to Wolfson College at Cambridge University.

Nicky Hager works as an investigative journalist and author. He has written six books about New Zealand politics, intelligence, public relations and military subjects. His most recent book was *Dirty Politics: How Attack Politics is Poisoning New Zealand's Political Environment*. He lives in Wellington.

Ross Nepia Himona. A retired sometime poet and occasional essayist, Ross was raised in country Hawke's Bay and in 1962 joined the army straight out of school. Commissioned into the Royal New Zealand Infantry Regiment, he saw active service in Borneo and Vietnam. He retired in the rank of major in 1982 and spent the next thirty years working in community and Māori development. In 1988 he started writing his popular 'Te Putatara' newsletter as 'commentary and opinion for the kumara vine'. It is now the online blog where 'Some Thoughts on ANZAC Day' was first published.

Ali Ikram is a writer and broadcaster based in Auckland. He has worked as a television journalist for CTV, TVNZ and most recently for TV3. In that career, he covered the Asian tsunami from Indonesia, the Coral Burrows murder inquiry and the Christchurch earthquakes. As a satirist, he wrote and performed the 'Week in Karaoke' song series and risked arrest to deface Labour's election billboards with the face of the party's own leader. His columns have appeared in the *New Zealand Herald*, *The Press*, the *Dominion Post* and the *Waikato Times*.

Lynn Jenner practised as an educational psychologist and counsellor for thirty-odd years. Her reading life was always noisy and
insistent. At the age of 49, she gave in to the temptation to learn to
write and think about books all the time. Jenner's first book, *Dear
Sweet Harry* – 'the autobiography of an obsession' – won the NZSA
Jessie Mackay Award for Best First Book of Poetry. Her second
book, *Lost and Gone Away*, deriving from her PhD thesis with the
International Institute of Modern Letters, was published in 2015 by
Auckland University Press. Lynn Jenner lives in Raumati and can be
found online at pinklight.nz

Elizabeth Knox has been a full-time writer since 1997. She has published three autobiographical novellas, ten novels for adults, three
novels for teenagers and a collection of essays. Her best-known
books are *The Vintner's Luck* and the Dreamhunter Duet
(*Dreamhunter* and *Dreamquake*). Her latest are *Mortal Fire* and
Wake. Elizabeth lives in Wellington with her husband, Fergus
Barrowman, her son, Jack, and three cats.

Tina Makereti is a novelist, essayist and author of short stories.
Her first novel, *Where the Rēkohu Bone Sings* (Vintage, 2014), has
been described as a New Zealand classic and 'a remarkable first
[book that] spans generations of Moriori, Māori and Pākehā
descendants as they grapple with a legacy of pacifism, violent dom-
ination and cross-cultural dilemmas'. It recently won the 2014 Ngā
Kupu Ora Aotearoa Māori Book Award for Fiction. Her short story
collection, *Once Upon a Time in Aotearoa* (Huia Publishers, 2010),
also won the Ngā Kupu Ora Māori Book Award for Fiction, in 2011.
In 2009 she was the recipient of the Royal Society of New Zealand
Manhire Prize for Creative Science Writing (non-fiction), and in the
same year received the Pikihuia Award for Best Short Story Written
in English. Makereti is Curator Māori for Museums Wellington
and convenes a Māori and Pasifika Creative Writing Workshop
at Victoria University. She is of Ngāti Tūwharetoa, Te Āti Awa,
Ngāti Rangatahi, Pākehā and, according to family stories, Moriori
descent.

Kirsten McDougall's first novel-in-stories, *The Invisible Rider*, was published by Victoria University Press in 2012. She was the recipient of the Creative New Zealand Louis Johnson New Writer's Bursary in 2013. She lives in Wellington.

Kristen Ng writes the blog Kiwese (kiwese.co.nz), with a focus on creative minds and cultural identity in China and Aotearoa. Born in Wellington, Kristen is a descendant of Poll Taxed migrants. After a traditionally Pākehā gap year in England, she gained a BA, double majoring in English Literature and Chinese, at Victoria University of Wellington, before returning to the Motherland in 2013 on a scholarship to Beijing. An avid supporter of independent music, she is often found in mosh pits, or diving on top of them. Kristen is currently writing and freelance translating in Chengdu. This is her first published work.

Joe Nunweek was born and raised in Auckland, but now lives in Melbourne, Australia. He is a founder and co-editor of arts and culture website *The Pantograph Punch*, has written for a range of other publications including *Real Groove*, *1972*, *The Spinoff*, *Overland* and *Sunday*, and has also been an itinerant producer for Radio New Zealand and 95bFM. Following a period practising community law, he is currently working in legal publishing.

Jenni Quilter's most recent book is *New York School Painters and Poets: Neon in Daylight* (2014), which charts collaborations between writers and artists in New York from the 1930s to the 1970s. She is a clinical assistant professor at New York University, where she also runs the Office of Global Awards. She is currently writing a collection of essays about, variously, Alexander Bell, American Sign Language, George Schneeman, Jane Bowles, Anders Breivik, Anne Frank, female bodybuilding, Iceland, Larry Rivers, Flight MH370, North African piracy in the seventeenth century, silent cinema, *The Virgin Spring*, Thomas Edison, Wilfred Thesiger, willy-waughs and Zeno's paradoxes.

Sylvan Thomson is a writer currently living in Invercargill.

Giovanni Tiso is an Italian writer and translator based in Wellington. He writes a regular column on media and memory for the Australian literary journal *Overland* and blogs at Bat, Bean, Beam.

Matt Vickers lives in Wellington and holds a management role at a global software company, which keeps him busy most of the time with work and travel. His blog, Lecretia's Choice, was written while his late wife, Lecretia Seales, underwent a High Court case to attempt to establish the right to choose the time and manner of her death under New Zealand law. Matt completed an MA in Creative Writing at the International Institute of Modern Letters in 2003.

Ashleigh Young grew up in Te Kūiti and now lives in Wellington. Her poems and essays have appeared in print and online literary magazines, including, most recently, *Sport*, *Griffith Review*, *Five Dials* and *Cordite*. She won the 2009 Landfall Essay Competition and the 2009 Adam Foundation Prize for her manuscript essay collection. Her book of poems, *Magnificent Moon*, was published in 2012 by Victoria University Press. On her blog Eyelash Roaming she writes about memory, mental health and cycling, among other subjects. She works as an editor and co-teaches creative science writing with Rebecca Priestley at the International Institute of Modern Letters.

Acknowledgements

'In ordinary life we don't spend very long looking at things
or at the natural world, or at people, but writers do.'
– James Wood, *The Nearest Thing to Life*

We are grateful to all the writers in this collection for looking at
things so closely, and we thank them for permission to republish
their fearless observations. We acknowledge the generosity of the
editors who first published these pieces, among them Ann Shelton
at *Enjoy* journal; Sarah Illingworth at *Impolitikal*; Simon Wilson at
Metro magazine; Joe Nunweek and Rosabel Tan at *The Pantograph
Punch*; and Marcus Stickley at *The Wireless*. Many thanks also
to Jude Tewnion and Fairfax Media; full credit to *Booknotes
Unbound*, *Overland* literary journal, *Landfall* and The Ruminator.
And a special thank you to John Campbell, who knows a good
story when he sees one, and whose jubilant prose energy makes a
perfect starting point to the book.

We're immensely grateful to the team at Auckland University
Press, Sam Elworthy, Anna Hodge and Katrina Duncan, whose
shared wisdom and expertise made this book possible; and to
Rebecca Lal, for proofreading it. We thank our 'anonymous
reader', whose thoughtful comments helped consolidate some
hard editorial choices. Once again our cover is adorned with an
elegant design by Philip Kelly – we love the way he makes us look.

Finally, thank you to our family and friends and all the
editors, writers and fellow readers who helped further our
reach and broaden our catch. If we'd been able to include every
recommendation, this book would be as wide as it is tall.

We welcome your correspondence: find us at TellYouWhatNZ@
gmail.com, or on Facebook and Twitter as @TellYouWhatNZ, and
tell us what you're reading.